Contents

Acknowledgements

We are grateful for the following permissions: A & C. Black for *Reading is Feeling* in Chapter Five; BBC Enterprises for the miscue chart in Chapter Three; Open University Press for summaries of Trevor Cairney's activities in Chapter Five; Random House Century for the extract from *The Sniff Stories* in Chapter Five; United Kingdom Reading Association for permission to reprint parts of Chapter Three and the British Psychological Society for material in Chapter Two.

Michael Jones assisted in the compilation of poetry lists (Chapter Six); Doug Dennis provided material for the Classroom Observation Checklist and Samanda Othen advised on the Key Stage 2 pen-portrait. Both in Chapter One.

Assembly of Chapter Seven depended upon the co-operation of numerous publishers and organisations as well as general advice provided by Diana Bentley. More specifically, Angela Redfern supplied information for the section *Professional Storytellers* and Rob Crompton for *Computer Software for Developing Reading*.

We would also like to thank the staff and children of Faringdon Infant and Junior Schools for the illustrative material used in Chapters One, Three and Five.

We are particularly grateful to Christine Adamson for her secretarial assistance and to Michael Lockwood and Betty Prescott for meticulously checking manuscripts for accuracy and coverage.

Introduction

The first two editions of *A Question of Reading* (1975 and 1980) were written in a totally different climate of primary schooling in general and the teaching and learning of reading in particular. This new edition is not a revision – it has been completely re-written to take account of both the National Curriculum *and* the debate about how reading competence should be developed in the primary years. Despite rapid changes in recent years we believe that the principles and practices outlined in this book will retain their currency well into the 1990's partly because they derive from rigorous research and partly because they have been tried-and-tested in schools.

A Question of Reading has been written with a dual audience in mind: primary practitioners *and* intending primary teachers. We have attempted to include much material which will give practical support as well as outlining and interpreting relevant research and theory, always within the framework laid down by the National Curriculum.

The book is arranged in a sequence which differs from earlier editions. We begin with classrooms (Chapter One) because, according to HMI, their organisation and management are the keys to the successful development of reading. Next we offer a rationale grounded firmly in research (Chapter Two). Then, because monitoring progress lies at the heart of the planning process, we position Chapter Three before two chapters which focus on reading in infant and junior classes (Chapters Four and Five). It should be remembered that this distinction is by no means exclusive – there will always be children who have not yet begun to read independently by the age of seven because the *normal* range for beginning reading extends to age eight or even nine. Likewise there will be children who read with greater fluency than the norm (e.g. infants who attain N.C. Levels 3 or 4) and who therefore require more challenging reading activities. Finally we consider those reading resources which will best foster successful reading (Chapter Six) as well as currently available support and advice (Chapter Seven).

Throughout it is important to bear in mind what the Cox Report

(DES/WO 1989a, 16.1) asserted about attainment in reading covering *three* related forms of development:

- the development of the ability to read, understand and respond to all types of writing;
- the development of reading and information retrieval strategies for the purposes of study;
- the development of knowledge about language.

Cliff Moon and Bridie Raban
January 1992

CHAPTER 1

How can I organise my class for successful reading?

We begin with two pen portraits of different classes:

1. A mixed-age infant classroom

Providing an efficient and effective learning environment for children in Years R, 1 and 2 takes careful planning. Firstly, the room is organised in such a way that children can move between different kinds of activities. Secondly, resources have been carefully selected to meet the needs of a wide range of skills and abilities. This wide range needs to be met even when children are all of the same chronological age. Children enter school with different degrees of understanding. Their learning has taken place at different rates and development has frequently been idiosyncratic. Because of this variation in individual levels of achievement, the class teacher plans activities which provide the opportunity to observe children as well as to spend time with the whole class and with individuals.

The classroom itself is the place where teaching and learning occur. Frequently we have to take account of architecture and furniture, and these conditions may determine how we plan the classroom. This classroom is organised so that a variety of activities can take place, care being taken to keep quiet areas furthest away from those which will always generate more noisy activities.

A focal point is the book corner, placed exactly where its name implies. Having shelves and book display furniture on two sides at right angles gives a feeling of privacy which helps the children as they browse through different books. This area is carpeted and has other soft furnishings like cushions and an easy chair. The chair provides a place for other adults to sit and read to and with some children while others are engaged with different activities. Areas are provided for writing as well as speaking and listening.

1

The role-play area/corner provides contexts for talk. However, listening needs a particular place which is quiet and this classroom is equipped with tape-recorders and headsets. Children listen to stories read aloud or other tapes made by the teacher and the children themselves. Some tapes are about how to play a game, others explain an activity the children are to complete for themselves. At the writing desk different kinds of paper are provided for writing, different pens and pencils, as well as a notice board above the desk for messages. Parents, teachers and children all leave their messages here, providing authentic material for the children to read and the teacher to read aloud. Next to the writing desk, the computer provides the opportunity for the children to compose directly and to screen or to prepare their final draft for publication. Care is taken to place the computer away from the window so that the screen is easily viewed; also it isn't facing the rest of the class so that the children and others working there avoid distractions.

Alongside these areas, there are others which provide space for maths work as well as science and displays of current work. Art equipment is readily available and musical instruments are stored where children can find them when necessary. However, the focal point of any infant classroom is the book corner. This is where books are read aloud, where children's own books are shelved for sharing with others and where guests to the classroom are invited to share books with the children and are made to feel comfortable and at ease. Sometimes the teacher uses this area to take their whole class work; sometimes it is kept as a quiet place.

Much of the work is centred on themes which are associated with topics that have been discussed and developed by all the staff. One example is referred to as *Using Children's Books*. Each staff member has selected a children's book and prepared a scheme of work to cover the English curriculum as well as other curricular areas. Each scheme of work has been designed to last two weeks, giving a whole term's work prepared by these six teachers, as each book and related project work is shared with every other class.

One example of this approach to integrated work has been based on the book *The Lighthouse Keeper's Lunch* (Armitage, 1977). A central focus for the project starts with the teacher reading this story aloud from a big book with the children and making sure that several small copies and tapes are available for the children to refer to in the book corner. The story is read aloud and discussed as each event in the narrative unfolds, taking care to relate these events to the children's own experience. The discussion around the story is important because the work which has been designed to follow the story reading requires the children to understand how their own activities are located within the fabric of the narrative.

In this story something happens on each day of the week and the writing area sees a group of children making their own diaries and writing an entry for each day. Another group of children are recounting the ways in which the gulls were thwarted in the story and they discuss other ways which might have been tried as well. A whole class activity which continues throughout the two weeks invites children to bring in objects which begin with **b** to put in the **b**asket which carried the lighthouse keeper's lunch, and also pictures of **l** objects to stick onto the **l**ighthouse picture. These words are reviewed every other day with all the children together.

In another part of the classroom, a group of children are making models of cottages and a lighthouse with a pulley system for the basket. They are testing out the strength of their design by putting different model foods in the basket. They are hypothesising how heavy the basket can be before it falls into the sea. Two children have made a model telescope while others are making magnetic fish to put in the sea. In the maths area, two children are conducting a survey of all the children's lunch boxes, while two others are entering preferences into a data-base as they prepare to make graphs of favourite sandwich fillings.

Further maths work involves children in cutting up sandwiches into halves and quarters, squares and triangles, with the youngest children counting how many magnetic fish they can catch. The model lighthouse is providing opportunities for some children to measure the dimensions and others to place in order of size different cut out pictures of lighthouses which have been collected from literature provided by the Lighthouse Keepers' Association. In geography, another group of children are inspecting the keys of different maps to find the sign for a lighthouse. They then count the number of lighthouses they can find around the coastline of Britain.

In science, children are learning how to light up the lighthouse with a torch bulb and a battery. They are discussing the dangers of electricity with their teacher and finding out how to send messages in code by flicking the light on and off at different intervals. Some children use their diaries to record the weather each day and others use the telescope to compare what they see with and without it. Using a mirror, the light from the lighthouse can be reflected in specific directions and this work leads into a discussion of other sources of reflection, as well as the power of a mirror to duplicate images.

Work of this kind can take many directions, but central to all the activities will be speaking, listening, reading and writing. Talking provides the opportunity to get ideas sorted out and writing provides a rich resource for children's reading. As well as this, books offer stories about other related events and reference material for information. Even at the simplest level of looking at books for pictures of familiar or new and interesting things, books are seen by the children as sources of stimulation and verification. For this reason, the book displays and the book stock take a prominent place in the classroom.

Each day sees books being read aloud to children, either by visitors to the class with individuals or small groups or, of course, by the teacher to the class as a whole. These are sometimes the children's own-made books as well as published ones. These times are opportunities for children to see how books are read and to find out what the print says if they cannot read for themselves. By knowing what the book is about and remembering the reading aloud trace in their minds, children can move a long way towards reading for themselves if favourite stories and accounts are returned to frequently enough and if the reading aloud is accompanied by discussion and support. Big books offer a way of sharing the text with a group of children and this resource usually has smaller versions of the book for display and browsing in the book corner.

While different groups of children are engaged in different activities, the teacher works with one group in particular, although there are some times when it is possible to observe the children without intervening too directly. These are opportunities for noting the ways in which different children learn in a group or on their own. While sitting at one table with children working, it is possible to listen in to another group of children. These are times when monitoring of children's learning behaviour is possible. Notes are made of children's ability to join in with a group constructively, levels of concentration are noted as well as how effective one particular grouping is.

Individual contact with children needs to be carefully planned. Time is set aside to spend with each child to discuss their work and to hear them read. Hearing children read will not always be from a book, but frequently for the youngest children, it will be from their own beginning writing or from a group piece to which that child has contributed. Talking to children about their work is the opportunity for making the next step in reading and for gauging the level of understanding reached. These are opportunities for monitoring progress through conferencing and must happen frequently, daily for some children, and two or three times a week for all of them.

The infant classroom is a busy place and it does not run on its own. The room itself needs careful planning, the resources need to be chosen to support the curricular activities and time management will need careful attention. There will be whole class activities like PE or watching a TV programme, there will be individual work and group activities. In order that this flows smoothly from activity to activity throughout the day, children need to be rehearsed in where things are kept and how to find out the information they need. Labels and signs around the classroom help with this as it involves the children reading from notices and messages as well as engaging in explanation and listening to instructions. As the older children take on more responsibility for their own learning, they begin to take turns in sharing their expert advice for the benefit of younger children. They know their way round the classroom and how things are organised and they learn from taking the role of expert.

Planning starts with *content*. With curriculum documents now in place, planning topics which cover the core and foundation subjects is a sophisticated activity. These schemes of work help to identify what is to be covered, but this does not deal with how the teaching is to take place. These decisions are taken by each teacher and require another stage in the planning. Further planning is also necessary to ensure that monitoring of individual strengths and weaknesses not only takes place, but that such monitoring supports further teaching decisions.

Classroom organisation checklist

The English National Curriculum non-statutory guidance (NCC 1989, 1990) identifies four main considerations to bear in mind when addressing classroom organisation. These are *classroom arrangement*, *resource management*, and the *management of people* and *space*. It is also stressed in the English curriculum that reading should be treated as an integrated language mode. This means that we see teaching and learning to read as embedded in speaking and listening as well as in writing activities. Learning to write will support the children in their development towards paying close attention to the letters or words on the page, while speaking and listening will support their use of syntactic intuitions in reading and give them knowledge about stories and the ways in which writing differs from spoken language.

Classroom arrangement

(1) For Speaking and Listening:

- a quiet area
- role-play area
- story-telling area
- listening area with tape recorders
- space for discussion with groups and whole class
- space for the children's presentations.

(2) For Reading:

- a print environment with labels, captions and notices
- space for reading – individually, in pairs and in small groups
- place for children to read to an adult

(3)   For Writing:

- a designated writing area
- writing display and message board
- word processing facilities
- book-making area

Resource management

(1)   For Speaking and Listening:

- access to TV/video
- availability of tape recorders
- computer
- telephone
- puppets
- dressing-up box

(2)   For Reading:

- books well displayed and accessible
- range of fiction and non-fiction
- different media (maps, comics, photographs etc.)
- children's writing
- word books, picture dictionaries

(3)   For Writing:

- supply of different writing materials
- examples of different writing
- word processor
- notice board
- book making material

People management

(1)   For Speaking and Listening:

- other adults as audience
- people to send messages to
- audience for presenting

(2)   For Reading:

- adults as readers
- adults as listeners to reading
- adults sharing reading

- children sharing reading
- parental involvement

(3) For Writing:

- adult as scribe
- people as focus for writing (e.g. letters)
- teacher as writer

Space management

(1) For Speaking and Listening:

- use of library, hall, corridors
- use of locality
- use of other parts of the school
- use of other schools

(2) For Reading:

- school library
- local library
- local environment

(3) For Writing

- use of other parts of the school
- use of other schools

QUESTION

Are you reviewing your own classroom and schemes of work for teaching reading within the English curriculum? It may be helpful to consider a checklist like the one above to ensure that a variety of options are available in your class for the children's reading development.

---

2. An upper junior classroom

The class of years 5 & 6 children are working, in groups, on various activities linked to a term's project on 'Victorian Britain', a History Core Study Unit at Key Stage 2. Their teacher has integrated this history-based project with 'Inventions and Energy Sources' in Science and 'India' in Geography. A range of mathematical work has been set into the context of Victorian life and the theme of inventions has generated plenty of Design & Technology potential. The teacher recognises that this whole-curriculum approach to planning will provide relevant and coherent teaching and learning opportunities for her children and, by designing tasks which pose problems for groups to solve, she knows that the children will have to collaborate and discuss at each stage of their learning. A good deal of the writing in which the children engage arises from the project and they have been encouraged to collect artefacts which are labelled and annotated in a 'museum' section of the classroom.

Already we see the potential for a variety of reading activities – reading assignments set by the teacher, consulting reference books and reading the museum annotations written by peers. In fact, most of the 'information retrieval' skills required by English AT2 are being well developed because of the way the children's work patterns have been established. The school has recently started collecting sets of non-fiction which support the project themes in its four-year cycle of projects which cover Key Stage 2 *content* requirements and the teachers have devised grids which enable them to check their coverage of learning *processes* as well as cross-curricular themes and dimensions (equal opportunities, world of work, etc.).

Apart from the project as a vehicle for information-retrieval (or 'study skills') the teacher ensures that half-an-hour is set aside each day for silent reading, drawing on an attractive class library of picture books, fiction, poetry, folktales, myths & legends and non-fiction. Some of these are shelved separated by genre, others are readability colour-coded to provide guidance for the children who are working within Levels 2 and 3 in terms of reading fluency. Once a week the teacher sets individual, paired or group tasks which are designed to foster reflective response to fiction reading (explorations of character, plot, motives, etc.) and the children also complete reading record forms, designed by themselves, when they have finished reading a book. These forms are mounted on a special 'Bookworm' display and later filed alphabetically by author surname in a ring binder which is kept in the class library for general reference.

The teacher recognises that child-to-child recommendations are far more powerful motivators than those which are teacher-to-child so, in addition to written reviews, she organises a 'bookshare' session once a fortnight. This involves the children telling each other, in groups of four, about the book they have enjoyed most in the last two weeks. They summarise the plot, refer to characters and prepare a short appetite-whetting extract to read aloud to the group. The aim is for each child to 'present' the book, within 4–5 minutes, in such a way as to stimulate someone else to read it for him or her self.

But the teacher knows that she is the person who is most likely to broaden the class's reading horizons so each day she reads aloud to them – a serialised novel, short extracts from new books, poetry *and* non-fiction. She is broadening their horizons in more ways than one because, for those children who have yet to become fluent readers, she is providing models of a variaty of written language genres and styles which are often more complex than those they can currently read for themselves. At the moment she is reading Penelope Lively's *A Stitch in Time* in daily instalments but she has also been reading extracts from Leon Garfield and Charles Dickens as a way of providing insights into life in Victorian Britain.

In order to help her children learn from their reading the teacher organises a weekly text-based activity at two or three levels of difficulty. This is always related to the project theme and again involves a great deal of paired and group discussion. She believes that information-retrieval skills and strategies are best learnt within the context of on-going work using the reference books which have been provided to support that work.

The class computer is in use throughout the day with individual and group rotas drawn up by the children. A word-processing program such as PEN DOWN or FOLIO enables children to compose and re-draft whilst a GRASS or TOUCH EXPLORER PLUS database facilitates the organisation of project material. Currently the children are compiling a database on Victorian household occupations drawn from census material from the local records office. The teacher also provides programs which foster prediction and study skills. Whenever possible she obtains simulation programmes which link with the term's project.

The class regularly watches the Thames TV broadcast *Middle English* and a viewing group joins other upper-juniors to watch BBC's *Look and Read* once a week with a parent who then supervises follow-up work designed by the school's Language Consultant.

Although SATs for this age-group will not commence until 1994, all the teachers have worked out procedures for continuous Teacher Assessment. As far as reading is concerned they keep notes (to headings) on each child's reading strategies, comprehension, information-retrieval skills, responses to literature, tastes and preferences. Additionally each child keeps a personal record of books read and enjoyed. Most of the notes compiled by the teacher are gathered during a 'reading conference' held with each child about twice a term. This is, in effect, a short discussion between child and teacher about reading habits and preferences with the teacher asking questions which will reveal how much has been appreciated/understood. For the less fluent readers it includes some reading aloud during which the teacher notes the strategies the child is able to utilise. The child's strengths and weaknesses are then diagnosed and activities are provided to assist further development. Such children are also helped with curricular reading demands throughout the week and the teacher spends time with them individually at least once a week.

Parents are involved in the reading development of all the children, whether at the level of discussing their current reading or, for the less fluent, sharing a book with them for ten minutes each evening. Guidance is provided by the school for both kinds of support and the parents' resource area contains copies of *Books for Keeps*, 'Signal' publications and a selection of booklets published by the Reading and Language Information Centre, University of Reading.

QUESTIONS

How do these classes compare with your own?
What would you want to omit or add if you were to modify your own class organisation?

These pen-portraits of infant and junior classroom organisation and management of reading raise a number of issues for further exploration. They are expanded in the chapters which follow:

Chapter 2   Learning to read, parental support
Chapter 3   Assessment, monitoring progress
Chapter 4   Stages in learning to read, big books, writing, reading aloud, variety of cues, phonics, knowledge about language.
Chapter 5   Developing response to fiction
              Information-retrieval
              Readability colour coding
Chapter 6   Provision and selection of a range of books
Chapter 7   Educational broadcasts
              Computer software
              Publication
              Big books

CHAPTER 2

What happens in learning and teaching reading?

Reading development

Developmentally, a growing understanding of the nature and uses of print does not occur in a vacuum. It depends on living in an environment where print is important. It depends on interactions with print which are a source of social and intellectual pleasure for both children and those around them. Researchers have pointed out that awareness of forms, functions and uses of print provides not just the motivation but the backdrop against which reading and writing are best learned. The notion of 'emergent' reading, therefore, pays homage to what we know about children's interactions with the world of print around them, and the kinds of assistance and guidance which adults give during the pre-school years in directing children's attention to print and demonstrating its function. Teachers in schools have been learning from these lessons and in the most successful classrooms, they have been finding ways of replicating this kind of environment for their children, an approach which provides an appropriate and easily understood context for further instruction.

The likelihood that children will succeed in learning to read at school depends most of all on how much they have already learned about reading before they get there (Raban 1984, replicated by Wells et al. 1984). This finding is also reflected in research findings from other countries (Clay 1979a; Ferreiro and Teborosky 1983). What we have learned from these observational studies is that all children pass through the same pathway of development in literacy learning. Some children pass through these developments faster than others and the varying rates of development have been shown to depend on experience of print and the quality of feedback on the children's attempts to make sense of the print which surrounds them.

However, Margaret Donaldson (1989) and others (e.g. Stanovitch 1986) point out that children, on entry into school, need to be explicitly taught

11

how to make further progress in their development. Donaldson, for instance, points out that meanings in environmental print, like talk, are deeply embedded in reinforcing contexts and therefore children need direct teaching if they are to orientate themselves towards the more powerful forms of literacy where meanings are embedded in the text alone. This continuum of development moves from generalised notions of signs giving meanings towards the alphabetic principle which focusses specifically on the text alone.

Children's knowledge about reading

In helping children to begin to focus on the text, reading schemes, and some teachers, assume that all children have a working knowledge of the concept 'word' when they enter school but this is not necessarily the case. This view can make 'developing a sight vocabulary' a difficult first step for some children. It is suggested, for instance, that the key to the development of 'word' awareness may lie in children's continual exposure to print with the teacher drawing their attention to how speech maps onto written words. Also, the development and use of explicit phonemic awareness as another starting point is very often both too slow and too difficult for many children. Indeed, from this point of view success in learning to read depends firstly upon linguistic ability in general, and only secondly upon the ability to make knowledge of features of written language explicit, as in displaying phonemic awareness.

Margaret Donaldson and Jessie Reid (1982) have identified clearly the developments in thinking over the last thirty five years which have guided us in coming to understand how children learn to read. They review the work of Jean Piaget (1955), Jerome Bruner (1957) and Noam Chomsky (1957) and assess the impact of their notions on our understanding of the reading process.

In the first instance, Piaget's concepts of assimilation and accommodation, supported by his observational studies, give evidence of the active involvement of the learner with what is to be learned. In learning to read, for instance, as the child initially grasps the principle that the printed text and not the picture matters most, their progress falters – what they 'knew' before, no longer remains available to them. For instance, as they begin to process letter knowledge information, words they could previously read become apparently too difficult for them. In acquiring more sophisticated information concerning the way text works, children apparently regress and then progress very rapidly, and this recursive activity makes one-off testing a hazardous exercise. New knowledge is not accumulated in an additive manner, rather the already acquired knowledge structures are re-shaped and re-organised as learning takes place. This is why any straightforward linear description of learning to read is so elusive. Bruner's studies concerning his notion of *perceptual recklessness* illustrate how willingly we all make inferences from limited perceptual information. It is important to learn to make balanced judgements concerning our perceptual hypotheses and have these informed efficiently and effectively by sensory information. This combination of perceptual and cognitive mechanisms working in tandem helps us to cross roads successfully, drive round roundabouts and survive the rush hour traffic. With respect to reading this process underlies the ability to read both fluently *and* accurately using apparently very small amounts of visual information.

If we process too much visual information, our reading is too slow to easily process the meaning of the text. However, if we are perceptually reckless, we process too little of the visual information on the page and read inaccurately. Bruner has pointed out the crucial role of the teacher in developing this balance, in providing children with opportunities to explore different strategies to get this balance right, a balance which will change with the changing demands of different texts for different purposes.

The role of knowledge about language

Importantly, Chomsky identified the role of syntax in the development of both the receptive aspects of language: listening and reading. Syntax is the rule governed part of the language system, including both grammar and morphology – patterning at the levels of sentences and at the level of words – which helps us to map meanings onto spoken or written patterns, speech and writing. He hypothesised that our innate predisposition towards this rule-governed aspect of language behaviour enables listeners and readers to make sense of spoken and written language by using syntactic invitations. For instance, English language users 'know' that *the* . . . signals a noun is to follow, not a verb, nor a preposition. We can in this way process meanings directly because patterns in language are expected and anticipated stable conventions; they are neither arbitrary nor haphazard. With this predisposition to anticipate how a sentence will continue, we are able to test out hypotheses against the language used by those surrounding us. Children, while learning to read, are also able to use their knowledge of the way language works to help them sustain meaning in their reading. They are able to make use of top-down processes, making sense of reading and searching for meaning in the text while, at the same time, attending to the graphic display which provides them with bottom-up information, information in the form of print.

What is essentially being argued by Donaldson and Reid and by Keith Stanovich (1986) is that reading can no longer be seen as a product; it must be conceived of in terms of an evolving process. Stanovich eloquently describes the model we now have as one of interactive-compensation. We now understand bottom-up strategies working with top-down strategies and trade-offs between the two. These strategies balance the tension between what we think is on the page and what is actually on the page and these strategies alter in emphasis as we read more or less difficult texts.

The debate over reading development continues, however, and there is argument for the primacy of grapho-phonic information in learning to read. Evidence from Peter Bryant and Lynette Bradley (1985) suggests that children's phonological awareness is a pre-requisite for learning to read and on the other hand, there is also evidence from Ehri's work (1979) which points out that reading development itself facilitates phonological awareness. However, whatever the direction of causality, even if it is reciprocal, explicit knowledge of phonemic awareness and the ability to use that knowledge in reading text, are not the same thing. As yet we know little concerning how children learn to use this knowledge except through its direct application to authentic texts, and this again is where the role of the teacher is crucial. The teacher is the person who mediates between the child's phonemic awareness and how this knowledge can be applied to print in a variety of texts.

Influence of the home

Early studies of home influence on progress in learning to read indicated that social class was a strong predictor of later reading attainment. These studies included large numbers of children and focussed on gross categories of socio-economic class which depended on the occupational status of fathers. However, Stephen Wiseman (1968) remarked:

> Factors in the home are overwhelmingly more important than those of the neighbourhood or the school. Of these home influences, factors of maternal care and of parental attitude to education, to school and to books, are of far greater significance than social class and occupational status. (p. 227)

The research conducted by the Plowden Committee on Primary Education (DES 1967) also provided evidence of the importance of parental attitudes.

More specific ways in which parents influence children's progress in the acquisition of reading have been shown by studies which focus on details of the home environment. For example, Jana Mason's study (1980) of four year olds illustrated the ways in which pre-school children begin to understand how features of writing relate to speech through parental guidance in the home and elsewhere. Joyce Morris (1966) found public library membership and book ownership also significantly related to later progress in reading.

Margaret Clark (1976), commenting on her research of 32 young fluent readers, pointed out that it is crucial to continue to explore factors like parental perceptions of education and the support and experiences they provide, by using measures far more sensitive than social class, father's occupation, or the education of parents. In her study, Clark was able to identify some significant features of the home environment which were relevant to progress in learning to read. These factors included the warmth and interest shown by parents in their children's development and which she observed to be outstanding. Both parents expressed interest in their child's progress and welcomed verbal interaction with their child; both parents were avid readers and belonged to public libraries. Clark emphasised that the most important contribution of the home towards rapid development was to ensure that written and spoken language were shared within a warm and accepting social context.

Magdelen Vernon (1971) hypothesised that this kind of environment would emerge in families with well-educated parents who were successful. However, this hypothesis was not borne out by Clark's data, nor by data collected as part of the Bristol Language Development study (Moon and Wells 1979, Raban 1984). Data in Bristol were collected both naturalistically and through interviews during the pre-school period and illustrate the powerful influence that parental provision for literacy made on reading attainment at seven years of age, in contrast to parental teaching, regardless of social class or educational levels achieved by the parents involved.

Role of parents

Parental provision for literacy in the Bristol studies was exemplified by activities such as buying books, comics, pens, paper, crayons and the like. Visits to children's libraries were also a feature of this provision as was reading stories aloud. Don Holdaway (1979) has stressed that the most important discovery in his research was not only the reading aloud of stories, but also the reading-like and writing-like behaviours of the children he observed. He pointed out that a feature of these behaviours was that they arose naturally without the direction, or perhaps even the notice, of parents.

The parents in the Bristol study were interviewed when their children were five years of age. During the first two years of the children's school experience, homes were seen to continue to provide similar environments both before and during their children's early schooling. The measures of a general positive attitude to their children's education was also found to be related to children's progress in reading. The measures of the home environment during this early period of schooling gave a picture of the importance of continued parental interest and support for their children's developing skills and abilities.

Providing opportunities for sharing books, using paper and pencils and taking an interest in their children's experience of school were all found to be beneficial from the child's point of view. In those homes where these opportunities and interest in school were lacking, the parents were equally eager to see their children succeed in school. However, they failed to have any ideas about how to achieve their ambitions. It appeared that their own experience had not enabled them to develop an intuitive understanding of what would be required and, for fear of doing the wrong thing, many of them saw such activities as the responsibility of the school. This view has been reinforced by teachers in a study by Peter Hannon (Hannon and James, 1990).

However, Holdaway (1979) has noted, as others have done, independent behaviour on the part of children which is 'self-regulated, self-corrected and self-sustaining'. This finding is supported by the results of the Bristol study (Raban 1984) where measures of child interest in literacy appeared to be independent of parental provision for literary activities especially if this provision was unrelated to what the children were trying to do for themselves. Clearly all children born into a print culture will show some measure of adaptation to their environment. Nevertheless, the more specific context of the family and the subtlety with which literacy interpenetrates the lives of the parents will have a more far-reaching effect on the particular form of the children's adaptive responses.

For instance, Shirley Brice-Heath (1983) has shown that understanding is the context rather than the outcome of learning and while children are not ignorant of print when they enter school, their particular understanding of its purpose and processes may differ widely. Importantly, HMI (1990) identify continued parental support and involvement as a crucial factor in children's reading progress during schooling and they welcome the programmes which schools were developing to strengthen home-school cooperation which they observed taking a variety of forms.

Entering school

A survey (Lake 1991) of 1500 children tested at age seven to eight years old every year at the same time for the last twelve years, using the same test, has been published by a Buckinghamshire psychologist. The trends observed through these data suggest a significant increase in the proportion of slow starters rather than any general deterioration in reading standards across the whole population. Analysis of a number of variables pointed to significant factors outside the school for this finding. Most importantly, changes in the characteristics of the catchment area were positively related to changes in reading scores. These characteristics were a measureable deterioration in the quality of background experiences which the children brought to school.

In Michael Lake's study, within-school factors did include changes in school policy which influenced the scores of less able readers – interviews illustrated that these changes were made by schools as a direct result of the changing needs of new school entrants. A further related study of 257 Buckinghamshire children indicated that parental mediation and parental interest in young children's exploration of the world of things and ideas around then was being generally lowered. This lack of support for children's word experience in general and interest in literacy in particular is cause for concern.

Learning to read in school

With respect to young children learning to read in school, detailed regular observations of children in infant schools have been conducted, for instance, by Marie Clay (1979a) in New Zealand and Hazel Francis (1982) and Bridie Raban (1984) in England. Clay pointed out that there are critical aspects of learning to read which we do not fully understand and the teacher's role is best characterised as a facilitator or consultant, not as didactic expert. Clay stressed the contribution that children make to their own learning and her study indicated how teachers can monitor and shape the emergent reading behaviour of young children starting school. Clay urged that the first two years of instruction in school are critical for learning to read as this is the formation stage of efficient or inefficient behavioural systems. She underlined the importance of reading progress, but pointed out that these skills cannot be applied directly to the activity of reading unless the child has already learned to direct attention to the significant features of the text, and this kind of learning takes place through experience of print and appropriate feedback from the teacher.

> Observation of children suggest that they do not learn about language on any one level of organisation before they manipulate units at a higher level. (1975, p. 19)

Although many curriculum and published schemes imply that this is the case, Marie Clay then goes on to say,

> As children learn to read and write there is a rich intermingling of language learning across levels, which probably accounts in some way for the fast progress which the best children can make. A simplification achieved by firstly dealing with letters, then words, and finally with groups of words, may be easy for the teachers to understand, but the children learn on all levels at once.

Work by Dorothy Bishop (Bishop and Adams 1990) concludes that what needs to be emphasised is that language skills exert a major influence on reading progress and cannot be ignored. What children bring with them to learning to read is their skill as users of language. They already know that language makes sense and they already have powerful understanding of the way in which language is structured. They know the syntactic probabilities of English and giving them opportunities to use this knowledge in beginning reading will help them through the early stages towards fluency. Bishop and Adams argue that phonological proficiency is not the main determinant of reading acquisition, but a result of using these syntactic and semantic abilities which they claim are responsible for the major part of variation in reading ability. They are here pointing out the role of semantic and syntactic cueing systems which both support and focus the need for the use of grapho/phonemic cues as the child learns to read both fluently and accurately.

Developing reading concepts

However, in learning to read written language, children have to learn new language features which are not apparent in speech. For instance, experimental work by Carolyn Chaney (1989) suggests that learning to read enhances children's notions of what constitutes a word, implying that learning to read will contribute to children's developing understanding of the features of written language, rather than children needing explicit knowledge of these notions before they can learn to read. Further work by Joan Mason (1990) indicates that as children make continuing progress in processing word units, this then becomes the frame within which phonemic segments and successions of letter arrangements can be examined.

In Mason's study of 189 five to seven year old children, her findings support a developmental model which implies that children will continue to increase in their knowledge of concepts and that new concepts about print may be acquired before earlier concepts are fully mastered. It is precisely because of this lack of linearity in language learning that the Cox Report (DES/WO 1989) found it necessary to stress the need to see progress with oral and written language development as recursive. The recursive nature of reading and language development has also made assessment difficult within the ten-level framework of the National Curriculum.

Teachers are now taking account of the developmental nature of learning to read and are finding ways of adjusting and elaborating their teaching methods to accommodate a wide range of understandings of print which children bring with them into school. HMI (1990) have observed this and note that teachers use a mixture of methods which do take account of children's differing levels of experience and understanding of print. Because teachers are differentiating their approach, it looks like a mixture of methods being used. This is because a snapshot is taken in one class at one moment in time. Identifying different children's place on a developmental continuum and providing appropriately for them in busy classrooms is the current challenge for teachers in Key Stage 1 classrooms and one which teachers clearly meet with enthusiasm and skill.

Teaching reading

In an extensive review of research, Marilyn Adams (1990) illustrates that within every instructional method that has been studied there are pupils who learn to read thoroughly and others who experience difficulties.

Bryant and Bradley (1985) point out that while phonologically competent pre-school children in their study became unusually good readers, the converse did not apply. Indeed, phonological categorisation tasks at ages four and five years were poor at identifying children who would go on to have reading problems. Bryant and Bradley conclude

> results like these support our belief that learning to read and spell is a complicated business which involves a number of different skills, of which we are tapping only one.

Phonics

The beginning of phonemic awareness is centred in children's first recognisable words and is developed in one way through experience of nursery rhymes and appropriate games. Children's early knowledge of nursery rhymes seems to be specifically related to their development of more abstract phonological knowledge and of emergent reading abilities. Children need explicit knowledge about letters and sounds, but this instruction must take place in the form of storybooks, notes, charts, displays and other engaging activities which reveal and reinforce the patterning of text. All beginning readers need to be provided with a variety of language games and activities designed to develop linguistic awareness directly. For instance, children learn letter names through alphabet songs and the like. This is an essential first step in order that they develop a conceptual arena within which to place letter knowledge and ultimately phonemic awareness, whether that be visual or auditory knowledge.

Linnea Ehri (1979) showed that word awareness increases dramatically along with the earliest signs of emerging reading behaviour. For successful readers, their explicit phonemic awareness develops alongside their word recognitions skills (Tunmer and Nesdale 1985). Success rates are dramatic when activities which enhance phonemic awareness are included in reading instruction and Ingvar Lundberg and his colleagues (1988) clearly state what they mean by 'instruction' in this context. Such instruction includes engaging children in a variety of games and activities involving nursery rhymes, rhymed stories and rhyme production, segmentation of sentences into individual words, investigations of word length, clapping and dancing to syllabic rhythms and solving puzzles, and finally isolation and identification of initial phonemes, then word final ones, and internal phonemes. These latter skills are developed late and require an amount of cognitive and linguistic sophistication which some children do not possess at the infant school stage.

Concepts about print

The performance of children on tests designed to measure concepts about print has also been found to predict future reading achievement. Moreover, it is important to point out that an analysis of other measures of reading achievement and readiness indicate that such basic knowledge about print generally appears to serve as the foundation upon which orthographic and phonological skills are built. The reverse is clearly not true. Experience of print and increasing knowledge about print need to interact in productive ways so that the child comes towards stable conceptions concerning the way print works. An important part of this teaching programme will be to encourage reading-like and writing-like behaviours from the beginning rather than believing that children are not yet ready for reading.

Across evaluations of beginning reading programmes, emphasis on writing activities is repeatedly shown to result in special gains in early reading achievement. The ability to read does not emerge spontaneously, but through regular and active engagement with print and the language experience approach, where tutors scribe what children say, can offer bridging texts in this respect. The children know what the text is about because they generated it, and so they do not have to struggle for meaning. The challenges of writing with invented spelling require children to think actively about print. In constructing their own meanings they work hard to make their print marks make sense to a reader. Although their spelling at this stage is not conventional, their phonetic script is easily read both by themselves and by others. Clearly opportunity to write is a positive component of beginning reading instruction.

Reading recovery

A significant contribution to our knowledge of best practice in recent years has been the emergence of the Reading Recovery Programme (Clay 1979b). This prescription for teaching reading is initiated by a diagnostic survey of letter recognition abilities, knowledge of the structure and functions of print, word recognition abilities, passage comprehension, writing skills. The first two weeks of one-to-one tuition explore what the pupil already knows and then continues with a focus on real reading and real writing of authentic texts. Reading then follows with texts the pupil can read using the technique of re-reading known texts. Writing is the principal means for developing word analysis skills. A language experience approach to writing is used, although independent writing is encouraged as soon as possible. A wide variety of other activities are engaged in by the tutor and the child. These include learning letter identities, clapping out syllables and segmenting words into phonemes, pointing to words while reading, all taking place in a supportive and structured environment.

The important feature of this programme is that it is implemented *before* children experience failure. Children are identified during their first year in school and the 'recovery' programme is aimed specifically at six year old children. What is interesting to note are the features of the programme which rest on research understandings and current good practice. The teacher spends time identifying what the child already knows, reading and writing are developed together, children are supported in making developmental increments, reading from books children *can* read and writing for a *purpose* provide the material for practice.

Noting the unusual success of one school in the Follow Through programme in USA, an analysis was undertaken (Meyer 1983) to see if there was anything in particular that it had done differently - and there was. Specifically, it was found that pupils in this school had been frequently engaged in reading and interpreting stories from the very first day of entry to school. The single most important activity for building the knowledge and skills eventually required for reading appears to be reading aloud to children. Rather than reading a story straight through, however, it seemed especially important to engage children's active attention.

It is not just reading to children that makes a difference,

- it is enjoying the books with them and reflecting on each book's form and content;
- it is developing and supporting children's curiosity about text and the meaning it conveys;
- it is encouraging them to examine the print;
- it is sometimes starting and always inviting discussions about the meanings of words and the relationship of the text's ideas to the world beyond the book.

Parents and others reading books with children are especially valuable activities in this respect.

Holistic approaches

What can be seen here is a blueprint for an holistic approach towards children's literacy development. Reading is seen to be for meaning from the start while writing, on the other hand, focusses the child's attention onto the detail of print. The major problem in reading with using contextual cues alone for word identification is that they can be unreliable. Therefore, as many opportunities need to be taken as possible to draw children's attention to phonological cues as they emerge and become significant and this is the case in learning to write. However, in reading, phonological cues alone will also be misleading. Because of this, conceptualisations of teaching have moved from *teaching reading* to notions of *literacy development*, in which learning-to-write experiences play their part in bringing children's attention to words and letter patterns.

Teacher effectiveness

Turning again to what teachers do when teaching reading, we are reminded once more of the Bullock Report (DES 1975) which emphasised:

> that the teacher is the biggest single factor for success in learning to read and use language in school and that 'the quality of learning' is fashioned in the day-to-day atmosphere of the classroom through the knowledge, intuitions and skills of individual teachers.

Successful schools are characterised by systematic and planned series of activities, reading teaching that begins as soon as the children enter school, and firm but friendly teacher control over classes (Cane and Smithers 1971). However, the results of this study and others were seriously questioned by John Gray (1979, 1981). In particular, Gray suggested that infant classrooms are statistically rather 'weak' environments and that as a result, children's reading progress was only slightly related to practice. What Gray was identifying in his research pointed to the fact that infant teachers did not display a wide variation of practice and because of this it was difficult to discriminate between them statistically.

This finding has also been confirmed in the Bristol study. The within-school differences were found to be greater than the between-school differences. This suggested that schools as learning environments were more similar than the children who entered them. An alternative way of interpreting this finding is that attainment in reading is more strongly related to individual differences between children than to differences in learning environments provided by schools. Nevertheless, it is clearly not the case that schools contribute nothing to children's learning, rather it is the case that schools do not significantly change the overall rank order of children which is established right at the very beginning of schooling, by the wide variation in their levels of attainment on entry to school.

However, the most important observation reported by HMI (1990) indicates that the majority of schools do now appear to be overcoming this variation. They make reference to characteristics of schools which mark out those with high standards of reading: firm leadership from the headteacher, a language coordinator, a school reading policy, classroom practice which reflects this policy and a wide variety of appropriate resources.

Factors influencing progress

In focussing on what schools plan and do, Lake's study reminds us that schools have had to pay particular attention to the changing in-coming characteristics of new entrants. Jeanne Chall and her colleagues (1990) at Harvard University followed the reading progress of children from low-income families to specifically explore this development. This study was characterised by the rigour and detail typical of the scientific research paradigm which she prefers. What is particularly interesting about this study is that her team joined up with a further research team led by Catherine Snow (1991) who researched the same children at the same time using an ethnographic paradigm. These teams of research workers have published their results in separate books and each report similar findings.

Both Chall and Snow observed children from low income families in a follow-up study. Data for the study were collected through classroom observations, teacher questionnaires/interviews and interviews with the children's families. They looked at the following variables in relation to the children:

Word recognition, reading comprehension and vocabulary (word meanings).

They identified the main characteristics of the children's school environment by studying the following dimensions:

- structure and organisation – both of the reading programme and the classroom. The teacher was seen to be businesslike and task-oriented and lessons were well-balanced, not constrained by a single scheme or approach;
- high-level skills – these were those activities which focussed on an understanding of what was read. For instance, talking about books read both by the children and the teacher, coupled with discussion in which word meanings became a focus of attention;
- enrichment – characterised by wide reading and related activities such as trips, library visits etc.

Opportunities were observed for writing and reading 'real' books and there was a wealth of materials in the classrooms including approximately 600 books, comics, encyclopedias etc. Reading and writing were seen to be continued at home. The level of diffiulty of the materials to be read was constantly challenging. There were opportunities to write at length and more difficult books were read aloud and discussed.

Strong positive relationships were found among the following combinations of variables:

- word recognition was influenced by structure and organisation of both the reading programme and the classroom, and by the challenging level of the reading materials;
- understanding of reading was equally influenced by structure and organisation as well as the enrichment activities which were provided by the teacher;
- word meanings were enhanced and increased through the challenging reading materials, high-level skills focussing on the meaning of what was being read and the enrichment activities.

As a result of these findings, Chall asks the question: What programme of reading instruction emphasis is best for children from low income families? She concludes; a reading programme that is goal directed, structured and challenging but also provides for wide reading of 'real' books – this kind of programme was observed to produce good results. For reading instruction, directed and guided by the teacher, the levels of difficulty of reading matter should be challenging – neither too easy nor too hard. This is an example in practice of Vygotsky's theory (1962) concerning what he referred to as the *zone of proximal development*. This theory informs us that learning is optimal when it precedes, rather than follows, the child's level of development.

Fluency was found to be a critical underlying factor influencing effective reading and wide reading was seen to be essential to the development of fluency. Importantly, time needs to be set aside in classrooms for reading, following taped stories, shared and paired reading. A low rate of vocabulary development was found to hinder later reading development and in order to hasten vocabulary development children need to hear challenging texts read aloud *and discussed*, but this activity must not be at the expense of children's own reading time. Vocabulary development was found to be assisted through children's own wide reading.

When contrasting approaches to reading between using reading schemes and 'real' books. Chall and her colleagues argue that either approach alone will not aid reading development. They have found evidence to support the view that children need access to the structure of a balanced reading programme, either published as a scheme or otherwise developed, along with the challenge and enrichment of wide reading coupled with experience of the world and opportunities for writing at length. Catherine Snow and her colleagues add that classrooms where solid gains were found in vocabulary development and reading comprehension were those with a rich variety of materials and activities used for literacy instruction.

Not surprisingly, children who were required to write at length became better writers and their reading comprehension improved. Therefore, these researchers suggest that more instructional time needs to be given over to writing, thereby giving children opportunities to compose their own texts and express their own ideas. In harmony with our own HMI report, one of the most robust findings from the research reported by Chall and Snow was the improved performance of children whose teachers were in contact with parents.

Time spent reading

One important variable in the school environment is the amount of time pupils spend on the activity of learning to read. Bamberger (1976) reports the findings of his study in terms of the paradox:

> Many children do not read books because they cannot read well enough. They cannot read well enough because they do not read books. (p. 61)

His point being that children become skilled readers through practising reading, by reading – not by thinking about it, talking about it, or doing exercises for it. Thus the pupil's 'time on task' is related to the essential need for practice in skill learning and this practice must provide the learner with feedback, an important element of which is seen as the teacher's guidance, interaction and intervention.

Cronbach (1977) pointed out that practice of a task was not sufficient to lead to success, and he also emphasised the need for guidance in relation to practice. He argued for 'an interplay among explanation, practice and further explanation'. The efficacy of this additional activity on the part of the teacher was reported by Stallings (1976) who conducted observations in 136 first grade classrooms. Factors relating to higher reading scores included the amount of time spent on reading activities and the time devoted to discussions about children's reading. Vera Southgate (1970) commented that the task of the teacher during such discussions was to help the child make the next step forward and point learning towards the ultimate goal of efficient reading. These findings suggest that it is essential to also consider the teacher's 'time on task' and how that time is spent in providing guidance for learning to read.

Variety of approaches

Regular observations of twenty children learning to read in infant classrooms (Raban 1979; 1984) suggest that those teachers who adopt a varied approach to learning to read activities, including a wide range of methods from the beginning, provide their children with greater opportunities for progress. How much time teachers devote to their pupils and pupils devote to learning-to-read activities, seems to be rather less significant than what they do during that time and, more importantly, the way in which the interaction and the task is shared by the teacher with each child.

The results of this investigation imply that differences between teachers are more subtle than any that had been previously systematically studied. While statistical analyses have been found valuable, they have little to offer our understanding of precisely what makes a difference for the child learning to read. We need to know more about what teachers do. What is needed is close observation and cataloguing of teacher behaviours across a range of classrooms in order to detect more or less successful strategies. However, HMI (1990) have indicated that older primary children working on Key Stage 2 require more time for reading than they observed.

Provision of resources

Research has indicated that the supply of appropriate materials for reading practice is positively associated with reading attainment. Joyce Morris' survey (1966) included analysis of the quality and quantity of reading materials in Kent schools and she found that poor standards of reading were associated with poor provision of books. Morris also evaluated the central library provision in these schools and found that poor readers were at a disadvantage with respect to the number of books available and the lack of suitability of their content. In a comparative investigation, John Downing (1973) found a wide range of variation in the provision of books in schools in fourteen different countries. In Denmark and Japan, where the teaching of reading was found to be particularly sophisticated, children had excellent book environments and the development of public libraries was also regarded as a powerful factor in the improvement of children's reading.

A study in Britain (Hodgson & Pryke, 1983) investigated a range of aspects of the teaching of reading in twenty Shropshire primary schools, including the provision and organisation of books. In the class of six year old children they found 30 per cent had books merely piled on shelves and found almost without exception that limited shelves and racks were insufficient to store books which were tightly packed and difficult to remove. Twenty five per cent of the schools appeared to lack care in the storage of books and 55 per cent of the books were found to be in poor condition and old in terms of publication dates, giving children out-of-date information. All teachers of the six-year-old children used reading schemes, with ten per cent of the teachers guiding children to use other books as well. Books from the school library service were generally not seen as an integral part of the reading programme and were of a high level of textual difficulty.

Quality of resources

More recently, it has been argued (Moon 1986, 1992) that attention be paid to the quality of reading experiences we offer young children as they learn to read. Reading schemes are still popular in schools, as publishers' sales figures will testify and HMI confirm. HMI report that 96 per cent of schools make use of published schemes. However, there is a danger that reading schemes can provide a straight jacket for children (Reed 1990) as teachers fall into the trap of leaving their own classroom organisation of resources and teaching of reading to the momentum of the scheme, rather than matching reading experiences to children's interests and their developmental needs. Jerome Bruner (1984) has pointed out that reading schemes seldom, if ever, contain material to which the child can respond emotionally yet that is the one experience which reading is best able to offer. This notion, coupled with that of Margaret Meek (1982) who claims that 'what the beginning reader reads makes all the difference to his view of reading,' makes any move towards a wide variety of books either alongside, or integrated with reading schemes, an obvious extension of appropriate school policy. In this way standards of quality and relevance are being raised in terms of the experiences provided for children in the environment of learning to read in school. Indeed, this debate has contributed successfully to the improvement of what publishers now offer in their reading scheme material. HMI (1990) note with concern, however, that provision of appropriate resources for older primary age children were not always managed or organised in such a way as to promote wide and effective reading.

Where next?

What is now required is close observation of practice in infant classrooms coupled with increasing knowledge of our children's entering characteristics, particularly as we begin to gain confidence in implementing the National Curriculum for English and the activities surrounding continuous monitoring and assessment.

28

Questions

- In what ways do teachers of reception infants take account of the knowledge of print which children bring to school?
- What needs to be the nature of the resources provided for children learning to read?
- How are these resources used and organised?
- How should teachers intervene to better facilitate children's reading in making progress with their reading and writing?
- How should we assess reading success?
- Which practices give rise to greater than expected achievement at seven years of age?
- What kinds of support would ensure that teachers facilitate children's reading effectively?
- What kinds of models of good practice can be shared with the profession at large?
- If reading standards are falling, what are the demographic shifts which might be precipitating this finding and how can they be counteracted in school?

CHAPTER 3

How should reading be assessed?

There is a passage in *Mrs. Frisby and the Rats of NIMH* (O'Brien, 1972) where Nicodemus describes how the rats were taught to read in the laboratory. Dr. Schultz and his associates first present the rats with individual letters, then words...

> I'm sure Dr. Schultz had plans for testing our reading ability. I could even guess, from the words he was teaching us, what the tests were going to be like. For example, he taught us 'left', 'right', 'door', 'food', 'open', and so on. It was not hard to imagine the test: I would be placed in one chamber, my food in another. There would be two doors, and a sign saying: 'For food, open door at right.' Or something like that. Then if I – if all of us – moved unerringly towards the proper door, he would know we understood the sign.
>
> (pp. 109–110 in Puffin edition)

A framework for national assessment

Assessment as defined by the TGAT report (DES/WO 1988a) may be any procedure, formal or informal, for producing information about pupils. This need for information about pupils is central to the implementation and purpose of the national curriculum and provides a sharp focus for recording and interpreting observations of pupil progress already made by teachers in busy classrooms. The TGAT report stresses that the assessment process itself should not determine what is to be taught and learnt. It should be part of the educational process, continually providing teachers with feedback on the success of their teaching strategies and information for future teaching plans. In view of this, teachers' records and assessments over time and in normal classroom contexts play an important part, and methods of assessment may often be incorporated into normal classroom activities.

The TGAT working group acknowledged that teachers typically use a wide range of sources to provide information for assessment; general

29

impressions, marking class work, pupils' self-assessment, rating scales, check lists, practical and written tests. The national system of assessment they proposed and which is now in place combines teachers' own records and assessment results together with the results of Standard Assessment Tasks (SATs). The TGAT report, therefore, provides a broadly-based framework for assessment which puts teachers at the centre of the process. The associated moderation procedures which bring groups of teachers together, provide a forum for producing the agreed combination of moderated teacher ratings and the results of SATs. Assessment procedures, at whatever level of formality, can only be useful in so far as they reflect the achievements of pupils and the closer these procedures are to everyday classroom activities, the more valid their results will be.

Assessment in the National Curriculum is required to fulfil four main purposes; formative, diagnostic, summative and evaluative. National assessment at the first key stage (7 years) is aimed primarily at identifying pupils in need of further support and serves a diagnostic and evaluative purpose. Formative information collected at each key stage is used to plan future work with pupils and only at the final key stage (16 years) does the assessment become summative. The formative aspect of assessment calls for appropriate profile reporting and the exercise of professional judgement on the part of teachers.

Development and assessment in English

The English working group (DES/WO 1989a) used these recommendations from the TGAT report to guide their own thinking on assessment in English. They acknowledged the inappropriateness of defining language development as a linear sequence. They stressed that language development is a process of refining competence as different aspects are returned to time and again with increasing sophistication. However, within this model of spiralling progress, they argue it is still possible to have expectations of pupil competencies at certain stages of schooling; for instance, when pupils change schools from infant to junior and onto secondary stage, when teachers and forms of teaching alter and new courses of work lie ahead. These are traditionally the occasions when teachers report to each other and parents concerning the competencies and progress of pupils. In view of this, the English working group argue that the requirements for national assessment at key stages makes current good practice both more explicit and common across all schools.

The English curriculum is now defined by profile components which are made up of attainment targets. These attainment targets are defined in their turn by ten levels of attainment described by statements of attainment. Their relationship is shown:

Profile Component	Attainment Targets	Statements of Attainment
Speaking and listening	1 Speaking and Listening	Levels 1–10
Reading	2 Reading	Levels 1–10
Writing	3 Writing	Levels 1–10
	4 Spelling	Levels 1– 4
	5 Handwriting	Levels 1– 4
	4/5 Presentation	Levels 5– 7

The way in which the profile components and attainment targets in English have been identified takes maximum advantage of the possibility for assessing pupil progress across the full range of primary classroom activities. Speaking and listening, reading, writing, spelling and handwriting all have a place throughout the integrated curriculum which characterises primary practice. These curricular opportunities for observing learning in English act as additional and supporting information to those records kept of progress through the English curriculum itself. In this way, needless duplication of records can be avoided. Indeed, the English working group stressed that spoken and written language competence is dependent on context with the implication that pupil responses to the widest range of tasks and variety of contexts will be required to achieve an adequate record of progress and accurate assessment. The group also stressed that forms of record keeping and assessment must pay attention to the process of accomplishing different activities using language as well as to the product of these events.

While the English working group agreed with TGAT's rough estimate of median levels of attainment at each key stage, they argued for a wider range of attainment around the median than TGAT proposed. They acknowledged that the learning process in English is characterised both by high and low levels of attainment unlike other content-based subjects. Therefore, they recommended a wider range of levels associated with each key stage:

Key Stage	Age	Median Attainment	Range of Attainment
1	7 yrs	Level 2	Levels 1–3(4)
2	11 yrs	Level 4	Levels 2–5(6)
3	14 yrs	Levels 5/6	Levels 3–8
4	16 yrs	Levels 6/7	Levels 3–10

Teacher assessment and SATs

Standard Assessment Tasks are the form of the external assessment required for reporting on pupil progress in the national curriculum at each key stage. They are designed annually to provide teachers with a package of different activities to choose from which arise out of familiar classroom contexts. They cover a variety of forms of presentation and require a range of pupil responses. More importantly, SATs can be conducted over an extended period of time rather than be confined to a short timed exercise. This form of assessment is standard for all pupils at the reporting ages and is needed to provide bench marks across schools and LEAs. Their results, however, are taken in the light of more detailed and continuous assessments which teachers make of individual pupils in the process of their normal observations and record-keeping.

Internal assessment requirements for the national curriculum will be based on those used by individual teachers and schools which centre on day-to-day record-keeping. This is the hallmark of informed primary practice. These procedures are both planned and structured to reflect the content of the English curriculum and its progression through ten levels of attainment. In order that this criterion is met, the assessment element of record-keeping is discussed and moderated with colleagues both within the same school and elsewhere. An example of this kind of record-keeping was suggested by the English working group. They identified the Primary Language Record (CLPE 1988) as a valuable starting point for teachers who are making their own records to reflect the profile components of the English curriculum and who now need to make their observations more explicit and available for other teachers and parents. In order to standardise internal assessments SEAC plan to develop a common national format.

The best record-keeping formats are those devised by teachers working together locally and fine-tuning procedures to their own pupils and relevant needs in relation to the curriculum objectives which are now nationally available. This, of course, is how The Primary Language Record was developed and it provides a useful discussion document for any re-evaluation or modification which is felt necessary to individual schools' current practice. Records of pupil observations and ways of interpreting these for assessment purposes are so inextricably bound up with the general processes of teaching and learning that they cannot be added on after decisions have been made about implementing the curriculum. Also forms of record-keeping will be a natural part of the discussions around pro-grammes of study and schemes of work.

Records of continuous assessment in reading now cover what has been read, reading strategies and approaches to familiar texts, levels of comprehension, retrieval of information and reading tastes and preferences. Miscue analysis plays a central part in identifying strategies and approaches to text as well as assessing comprehension. More importantly, techniques like these reveal profiles of strengths and weaknesses and differentiate between varieties of errors. In writing, internal assessment focusses mainly on the writing process as distinct from the product alone. This requires records of pupils' conferences where ideas for writing and drafts are discussed. Also samples of work at different stages of the process need to be collected alongside finished pieces. In particular, pupils' ability to reflect on what they are reading provides valuable information concerning their growing confidence and independence.

There is a danger that weak forms of internal assessment will give undue prominence to the results of SATs and this is to be avoided. It is only through the structured observations of teachers and their dated records of language events across a wide range of tasks and contexts that SAT results can be modified accurately to assess the attainment levels of individual pupils. When there is a discrepancy between the results of external and internal forms of assessment, the TGAT report comes down on the side of internal assessment. However, if the bases of these internal assessments are not sufficiently detailed and clearly structured to resolve the discrepancy unequivocally, then the results of SATs will be taken as final. Indeed, SEAC is making moves in this direction (Nash 1989) and it is, therefore, a matter of some urgency that teachers' own record-keeping and forms of internal assessment survive possible public scrutiny in the immediate future.

Reporting levels of attainment

The English curriculum is now defined by ten levels of attainment which are made up of statements which identify strands which run through the levels. A pupil achieves a level of attainment if all the strands in that level have been achieved. However, a pupil may be making progress with some of the strands in the following levels and these should be noted. Individual strengths and weaknesses will become clearer if this amount of detail in records is retained and will be particularly valuable information for sharing with other teachers planning future work and for reporting to parents.

Reporting to Parents	**School or LEA Profiles**
Level achieved for each individual attainment target and strands achieved at higher levels	Single score for English equally weighted for Key Stages 1 and 2. Aggregation of levels across Profile Components (percentage of pupils at each level to be reported)

The kind of information shared with parents and other teachers is very different from that made available concerning a school or LEA. Public scrutiny beyond the immediate context of the school and classroom is not of sufficient detail to reveal the achievements of individual pupils. More importantly, all documents concerning the national curriculum accept that there will be a period of time during which both the curriculum and these assessment procedures are tried in practice. The curriculum itself may well over- or under-estimate the progress which can be expected of pupils at different ages and only time and continuous monitoring will reveal any discrepancies which require modifications. The most essential evidence for these modifications will be teachers' continuous records of dated observations including samples of pupils' work across time. This kind of evidence is the major indication of the appropriate rates of development and progress.

Guidelines for the accumulation of evidence are given in the non-statutory guidance (NCC 1990) now available in all schools. The chart on page E4 gives a clear indication of what this evidence might look like. The three main areas of data collection for records are factual details, teachers' observations and samples or work. These are best collected under the headings of the five attainment targets rather than the three profile components as set out in the chart, although spelling and handwriting should never be assessed apart from more general writing purposes. Further records need to be kept of conferences with individual pupils and their self-assessments along with notes of discussions with parents. Cumulatively, these records serve all the necessary purposes of assessment:

• help in planning further work
• feedback and response for pupils themselves
• maintenance of curriculum coverage
• information for other teachers
• evidence for assessment at reporting ages.

Teacher assessment of reading at Key Stages 1 and 2

The guidance provided in the Cox Reports on what was then called 'internal' and 'continuous' assessment spells out clearly *what* should be assessed and *how* it should be assessed. There is a recommendation that the *Primary Language Record* (CLPE, 1988) might be adopted as a starting point, that assessment 'should not make excessive demands upon time or resources' and that it needs to commence when the child enters school, continuing throughout the primary years (DES/WO, 1989a para 16.46). Then, in addition to reviewing the 'strands' which constitute the Reading AT (and hence imply assessment) the guidance extends to the specific suggestion in the Cox Report that *miscue analysis* could be utilised to monitor the reading strategies used by a reader (para. 16.47).

The procedure known as 'miscue analysis' was researched and promoted by Kenneth and Yetta Goodman throughout the 1960's and 1970's. Goodman defines a miscue as:

an actual observed response in oral reading which does not match the expected
response. (Goodman, 1973, p.5)

For example:

TEXT   Sally went out to tea
READER   Sally went out today

Goodman claims that 'miscues' generated by readers (when reading aloud)
are 'windows on the reading process' and as such can help teachers
understand which strategies a reader has already learnt to employ as well as
those the reader could be encouraged to develop, with teacher support and
guidance.

The great strength of this approach is that it is a form of reading
assessment which takes place within the everyday classroom practice of
children reading aloud to teachers. The procedure developed by Goodman
was later simplified by Yetta Goodman and Caroline Burke (1972) and was
extensively disseminated by Elizabeth Goodacre in the U.K. (See, for
example, Goodacre 1976). Miscue analysis was an integral part of the
Extending Beginning Reading project (Southgate *et al*. 1981) and Chapter
16 of that project's report provides a useful introduction to the subject.
Helen Arnold (1982) subsequently developed miscue analysis with teachers
and set out a modified, step-by-step method with suggestions for at-a-glance
records based on a Venn diagram analysis of *substitutions* (e.g. 'house' for
'home', 'thought' for 'through').

Conducting a miscue analysis.

The generally accepted procedure requires that the teacher tape-records a
child reading aloud and subsequently marks a photocopy of what was read
with pre-determined symbols denoting the types of miscues made. The
marked passage is then analysed to demonstrate the strategies used or
under-used by the reader. Often the miscues are grouped according to
whether they are positive or negative. Positive miscues usually retain the
meaning of the original text, while negative miscues are considered to
usually detract from the meaning. After reading aloud the child is asked
either direct questions about the passage *or* is asked to re-tell the gist of
what has been read so that the teacher can assess how much of the text has
been understood.

There is some disagreement about whether the text should be known to
the child beforehand. The *Primary Language record* states:

> The selected text should not be well known to the child and should be one that
> makes demands of the reader without causing frustration. (CLPE, 1988,
> p.61)

We believe that for any assessment to be reliable, it must be as close as possible to normal classroom practice. We therefore suggest that miscue analysis should be conducted with the book the child is currently reading and wishes to share with the teacher during a 'reading conference'. Where this book is insufficiently demanding to trigger sufficient miscues for analysis, or where it is well beyond optimal reading competence, then the teacher can either postpone miscue analysis or suggest the child reads from a recently experienced alternative text which provides a better match. The Cox Report (DES/WO, 1989a, para. 16.47) sets out the four-fold procedure which then follows...

(1) The text should be read silently.
(2) It should be re-told or described by the child to the teacher.
(3) The text should be read aloud, with the teacher marking miscues on a duplicate copy.
(4) The text should be discussed in more detail with the teacher.

This account excludes the use of a tape-recorder, although it is highly unlikely that the third stage could be conducted satisfactorily without one unless the teacher had had a great deal of familiarity and practice with the procedure.

Code for recording miscues		
Sentence to be read	She was washing up in the kitchen	
Error type	*Coding*	*Example*
Substitution	Underline and write in the word substituted	*were* She was washing up in the kitchen
Non-response	Dotted line under the word if reader waits to be prompted or asks	She was washing up in the kitchen
Insertion	Add additional word/s or part-word added	*out* She was washing up in the kitchen
Omission	Circle word/s left out	She was washing up in the kitchen
Pause	Stroke, use when reader pauses for more than two seconds	She was washing/up in the kitchen
Repetition	Mark the word/s repeated with a curved line	*R* She was washing up in the kitchen
Correction	Write in original miscue, then curved line with the letter (c) for self-correction	© *had been* © *bowl* She was washing up in the kitchen

Table 1   (Goodacre, 1976, p. 107)

(This chart is reproduced from *Teaching Young Readers* by Elizabeth Goodacre, edited by Chris Longley, with the permission of BBC Enterprises Ltd.)

Most of the authorities referred to so far supply frameworks for coding and marking miscues. There is no single standard system but Elizabeth Goodacre illustrates a clear set of symbols (see Table 1).

Both *The Primary Language Record* (CLPE, 1988) and Arnold (1982) provide examples of marked up passages and their subsequent analysis, but Helen Arnold, in particular, emphasises the need to look more carefully at *substitutions*. She uses Venn diagrams to analyse similarities of substitutions according to three criteria:

- Graphophonic
- Syntactic
- Semantic

This derives from Goodman and Burke (1972) who analysed, amongst other criteria:

- Graphic similarity
- Sound similarity
- Grammatical acceptability
- Semantic acceptability

It appears that Arnold's conflation of 'graphic' and 'phonic' similarity into a single criterion is an attempt to facilitate the Venn diagram record. However there are instances where both fail to coincide especially where the initial sound is affected as this is the most revealing demonstration of phonic knowledge,

e.g. *ever* for *never* is graphically similar:

but as the initial letter is different it cannot be classified as phonically similar.

It is therefore desirable to classify substitutions according to all four criteria if we are to satisfactorily describe the reader's strategies:

- graphic   the shape and length of the word
- phonic   the sound of the word, paying particular attention to initial sound (then final sound)
- syntactic   the part of speech (e.g. verb for verb, noun for noun)
- semantic   retention of original meaning (e.g. 'house' for 'home', 'Mum' for 'Mother')

But why all this emphasis on substitutions? Research has frequently demonstrated that the most powerful information produced by miscue analysis is the quality and quantity of substitutions. For example, fluent adult readers substitute words a great deal (try reading aloud yourself to a colleague) but these substitutions are usually synonyms. It can be argued that the mark of a reader's fluency and confidence is the tendency to substitute semantically appropriate vocabulary. It is particularly interesting to note the relationship between frequency of substitutions and frequency of refusals (or 'non-responses') as an indicator of a child's confidence as a reader. The child who relies more on teacher assistance in supplying unknown words is less confident than the child who 'has a go' and substitutes words, *even if* the words substituted are inappropriate in the context of what is being read. Future planning for these two children is facilitated by further analysis, for example:

(1) *Reliant Child*

- teacher encourages prediction based on information available in text.
- teacher supplies cloze passages etc. to foster informed prediction.

(2) *Confident Child*

- teacher encourages closer scrutiny of substitutions which detract from original meaning.
- teacher supplies games and/or exercises which draw attention to cues not being attended to.

A variant form, but lacking the precision of miscue analysis, is the *running record*, devised by Marie Clay (1985). It is particularly useful with emergent readers who are 'talking like a book', reading the pictures but not yet able to make accurate or near-accurate predictions about the specific text which accompanies them. With such children the running record can give a great deal of objective information about the child's increasing orientation to independent reading. A concise account of the operation of running records is available in *The Primary Language Record* (CLPE, 1988, pp. 59–61) and infant teachers who carried out the SAT in 1991/92 will be familiar with the procedure as it was the means of assessing reading fluency and understanding at Level 2 (SEAC, 1991).

Miscue analysis in context.

A number of attempts have been made to contextualise the insights gained from miscue analysis, particularly in respect of miscue analysis as a component of a 'reading conference'. *The Extending Beginning Reading* report (Southgate *et al.* 1981) concluded that miscue analysis was one example of the activities which might be undertaken during 'longer, less frequent individual contacts with children'. Other examples included discussion of book preferences and reading habits, comprehension of what had been read, vocabulary extension, keeping notes/records and planning ahead. Valuable insights into 'conference' discussion before, during and after a read-aloud session have been provided in two transcripts by a junior school teacher, Anne Baker (1984 and 1985). The way that miscues can be triggered by textual inadequacies as well as guidance on teacher intervention during a child's reading to a teacher can be found in Moon (1984). Campbell (1988) outlines his research findings on infant children reading aloud to teachers and supplies a useful and practical list of twelve suggestions for teachers and parents who hear children read. He is particularly concerned about what he calls 'opening and closing welfare moves' and the provision of positive feedback.

Teacher assessment

It is against this background that we return to the recommendations of the Cox Committee. To begin with the report stated:

> For internal assessment, a common national format for record-keeping should be devised and employed. We recommend that SEAC, in consultation with NCC and CCW, develop an assessment format and handbook and that the approach exemplified by the *Primary Language Record* (1988, CLPE) be adopted as a starting point. (DES/WO, 1989a, para. 16.46)

Sadly a 'common national format' has not yet materialised and infant teachers receiving children from other schools during 1990 and 1991, in the middle of Key Stage 1, have found the disparities in Teacher Assessment records disconcerting and frustrating.

The report then went on to describe five facets of reading development which should comprise TA records:

> The record of continuous assessment should cover what the child has read; the child's reading strategies and approaches when handling a familiar text, levels of comprehension, retrieval of information, and the child's reading tastes and preferences.
> (DES/WO, 1989a, para. 16.48), identical in (DES/WO, 1988b, para. 9.22)

We shall deal with each of these in a different order, leaving 'reading strategies and approaches' until last.

1. *What the child has read.*

The purpose of this record is to ensure that children are having a broad and balanced reading diet based on the genres required by the National Curriculum: picture books, novels, nursery rhymes, poems, folk tales, myths, legends and non-fiction (see Chapter Six for full details). These genres define the word 'range' in Statements of Attainment at Levels 2, 4 and 6. Some infant teachers keep a large card index file handy and note books which have been read under date and title. Full cards, or photocopies of them, are attached to a summary record as evidence of range of reading and passed to the next teacher and, at the end of Key Stage 1, to the junior department/school. Older children can keep their own records of books read and enjoyed. These can be in the form of notebooks, logs or diaries, but increasingly schools are developing their own reading record forms which are designed to complement the term's project. A class might be asked, for example, to design reading record forms based on their own drawings of insect body parts during a project on 'minibeasts'. This not only involves the children in their own learning and recording but also introduces a valuable design activity. A wealth of starting points for records of this kind can be found in Gwen Gawith's *Library Alive* (1987).

2. *Levels of comprehension.*

In the past, comprehension was often assessed by passage-plus-question tests which were open to abuse and misuse. Traditionally many of the questions only required literal regurgitation and children soon discovered that rather than read the passage, the trick was to search for the keywords and re-formulate the question into a correct answer. The National Curriculum has other intentions which start with oral comprehension:

> Pupils should be able to demonstrate, in talking about stories and poems, that they are beginning to use inference, deduction and previous reading experience to find and appreciate meanings beyond the literal.SoA, Level 3(d).

This extends to 'non-fiction and other texts' at Level 4 but still involves talking, not writing.

The assessment of comprehension in the Level 2 SAT (SEAC 1991) required that the child tell the teacher what had happened in the story so far and then make a sensible prediction about what might happen next. At later levels this idea could be extended to asking:

> Suppose XXX had not happened in this story but ZZZ had happened instead. How might the story have ended differently?

Clearly questions like these are ideally suited to a 'reading conference' when discussion can centre on the particular book the child wishes to share with the teacher that day. Summary records then restrict the teacher's assessment of comprehension to a specific piece of evidence. A further way to monitor comprehension is to note the incidence of miscues which retain meaning during miscue analysis.

3. *Retrieval of information.*

This area of assessment relates to children's ability to:

Level 2 'Demonstrate knowledge of the alphabet in using word books and simple dictionaries'.

Level 3 'Devise a clear set of questions that will enable them to select and use appropriate information sources and reference books from the class and school library'.

Level 4 'Find books or magazines in the class or school library by using the classification system, catalogue or database and use appropriate methods of finding information, when pursuing a line of enquiry'.

Level 5 'Select reference books and other information materials and use organisational devices to find answers to their own questions and those of others'.

Obviously these skills and competences will be employed in the context of project and related activities especially when children are challenged to independently research information. Assessment is likely to centre on teacher observation as and when such instances occur.

4. *Tastes and preferences.*

As with 'levels of comprehension', discussion about tastes and preferences will usually take place during a reading conference. Indeed all reference to 'tastes and preferences' prior to Level 5 mention 'talking'. Only at Level 5 do we have:

> Pupils should be able to demonstrate, in talking *and writing* about a range of stories and poems which they have read, an ability to explain preferences.

Until this point, the Statements of Attainment which guide our assessment include:

Level 1 'Talk in simple terms about the content of stories, or information in non-fiction books' (The example adds 'including likes and dislikes.')
Level 2 'Listen and respond to stories, poems and other material read aloud, expressing opinions informed by what has been read.'
Level 4 'Demonstrate, in talking about a range of stories and poems which they have read, an ability to explore preferences.'

Typically an infant teacher might open a discussion with an individual or group after the class has listened to a story or poem, whereas a junior teacher might peruse a child's reading record and say:

> I see you enjoyed this book – what was it that you particularly liked? Why did

you like that character/event/ending? Are there any other stories you've read that you liked for the same reason?

This kind of discussion can lead to the teacher recommending further reading by the same, or a different, author/poet. The record will probably benefit from headings like authors, poets, genres and home reading – children might well have a different set of home preferences which relate to hobbies, television and family interests.

5. Reading strategies and approaches.

We were fortunate, during 1990–91, to have the opportunity to collaborate with an Oxfordshire infant school in its formulation of Teacher Assessment of reading strategies. The format itemised below was also found to be successful with juniors and is offered here as a suggested approach to assessment at Key Stages 1 and 2 for those children who are no longer 'emergent readers' and have not yet gained sufficient fluency to read texts in Stage 12 of *Individualised Reading* (Moon, 1992). In National Curriculum terms their fluency range would be from 'working within Level 2' to 'working within Level 4'.

The teachers we worked with had been trained in the use of full-blown miscue analysis but found it too time-consuming for normal classroom purposes, bearing in mind the demands of Teacher Assessment in other areas of the curriculum as well as in other English ATs. Yet miscue analysis seemed to offer the most useful insights for future teaching and learning. What ensued was a series of experimental recording forms, culminating in the one illustrated, which concentrated on just two miscue types – substitutions and refusals (or 'non-responses'). Even the latter are dispensable if you choose the speediest option because a qualitative analysis of substitutions alone will indicate the strategies a child is either using or under-using. See Table 2.

This concentration on substitutions echoes previous research on miscues which is described earlier in this chapter. The Programme of Study for Key Stage 1 states that:

> Through the programme of study pupils should be guided so as to ... use the available cues, such as pictures, context, phonic cues, word shapes and meaning of a passage to decipher new words.   (DES/WO, 1990, p.30)

And at Key Stage 2:

> Pupils should ... be encouraged to think about the accuracy of their own reading and to check for errors that distort meaning. (DES/WO, 1990, p.31)

The added advantage of the simplified miscue analysis is that it does not require a tape recorder, a condition stipulated by the school we were

DATE   NAME   CLASS   AGE   YEAR

TITLE & PAGE(S) OF BOOK

| SUBSTITUTIONS | | Similarity | | | |
Word read	Word printed	Sound	Look	Part of Speech	Meaning
1					
2					
3					
4					
5					
6					
7					
8					
9					
10					
11					
12					

Tally of refusals	

$$\text{Negative miscue rate} = \frac{\text{Add crosses in Meaning col. to no. of Refusals}}{\text{Total no. of words read}} \times 100 =$$

$$= \qquad \%$$

LEVEL = independent/instructional/frustration

           (1%)   (5%)   (10%)

NOTES ON MISCUE ANALYSIS

Table 2

working with. All the teacher has to do is note 'word printed' and 'word read' each time the reader substitutes a word during reading aloud. This has now been tried many times by different teachers and children in different schools and difficulties are only encountered if there is excessive background noise during the time the child is reading. A very important reading strategy is monitored as a by-product of this method: self-corrections are automatically recorded because the teacher has already written 'word printed' and 'word read' before the correction occurs. This obviously helps teachers to assess the ability of children to 'check for errors that distort meaning.' All other cues mentioned in the PoS are monitored (with the exception of pictures):

- context – 'part of speech' and 'meaning'
- phonic cues – 'sound'
- word shapes – 'look'
- meaning

After the reading is completed the teacher ticks and crosses the cells according to the *similarity* between 'word printed' and 'word read' (see examples) and then looks for patterns. Some observations are made here about two examples which are illustrated in Table 3 and Table 4. You may be able to think of others.

- Matthew's analysis shows that he is reading for meaning but that he needs to pay closer attention to phonic and graphic cues. The reverse applies to Gareth.
- Further confirmation of Matthew's attention to meaning cues is his self-correction. He read *little* as *small* but then self-corrected to *little*. Even if he had not self-corrected, *small* would have retained the meaning. Gareth also self-corrected (worked/walked) but there is a difference – the original substitution did not retain the meaning.
- The tally of refusals shows that Gareth is a more confident reader than Matthew who should be encouraged to predict unknown words rather than look to his teacher to supply them. The maxim is that: 'Tis better to have substituted and erred, than never to have substituted at all!'.

The numerical calculation is also optional but is useful for assessing the *match* between the competence of the reader and the readability of the text. Matthew's book is well within his competence whereas Gareth finds his more challenging. Matthew could cope with a slightly more demanding text, Gareth should gain more experience at the same level. The basis of the computation is the three levels of reading fluency developed many years ago and set out in the Bullock Report (DES, 1975). The definition of a 'negative miscue' for this purpose is refusals *plus* substitutions which fail to retain meaning. This is a short-cut method of calculating reading level, but from experience, it appears to provide a satisfactory indication. The number of

DATE 16.3.90   NAME Gareth   CLASS 3 AGE 7 YEAR 2

TITLE & PAGE(S) OF BOOK The Farmer and his sons
(Fables from Aesop)

SUBSTITUTIONS		Similarity			
Word read	Word printed	Sound	Look	Part of Speech	Meaning
1 gave	grew	✓	✓	✓	X
2 gold	great	✓	✓	✓	X
3 let's	let us	✓	✓	✓	✓
4 digged	dug	✓	✓	✓	✓
5 walked	worked				
6 piece	penny	✓	✓	✓	X
7 couldn't	could	✓	✓	✓	X
8 sons	soon	✓	✓	X	X
9 gave	grew	repeat	—	do not	count
10 money	market	✓	✓	✓	X
11					
12					

Tally of refusals	ЖН

Negative miscue rate = $\dfrac{\text{Meaning (X) PLUS Refusals}}{\text{Total no. of words read}} \times 100 = \dfrac{1100}{146}$

= 8 %

LEVEL = independent/instructional/frustration
(1%)   (5%)   (10%)

NOTES ON MISCUE ANALYSIS

Readability of book quite challenging
Think about meaning — cloze activities?
Plenty of confidence

Table 3

DATE 16.3.90   NAME Matthew   CLASS 5 AGE 7 YEAR 2

TITLE & PAGE(S) OF BOOK   Goldilocks and the Three Bears

SUBSTITUTIONS		Similarity			
Word read	Word printed	Sound	Look	Part of Speech	Meaning
1	small	little				
2	small	tiny	X	X	✓	✓
3	but	well	X	X	✓	✓
4	not	never	✓	X	✓	✓
5						
6						
7						
8						
9						
10						
11						
12						

Tally of refusals	ЖHT 1

Negative miscue rate $= \dfrac{\text{Add crosses in Meaning col. to no. of Refusals}}{\text{Total no. of words read}} \times 100 = \dfrac{600}{178}$

$= 3.4$ %

LEVEL = independent/instructional/frustration

(1%) ⌐   (5%)   (10%)

NOTES ON MISCUE ANALYSIS

Readability of book about right — suggest others in same series / at same level.
Encourage him to attempt words himself.
Some initial consonant work?

Table 4

words a child reads is variable – the best advice is to stop when the child tires (usually over 100 words) or when the child has read 400 words, whichever comes first.

Apart from its time-saving virtues, a further advantage of this approach is that almost any kind of text can be used at any time. So long as there is a piece of continuous prose and the child is willing to read it to you then you have a 'sample' or potential piece of evidence for assessment purposes. You can also fit the assessment into almost any kind of reading-time organisation. If you normally share a book, taking turns to read, then jot down the substitutions made when it's the child's turn – the sample of reading may be from two or three passages in the book as the recording procedure does not depend on a single uninterrupted passage read by the child.

So the method we have outlined is very flexible and is designed to fit in with normal, everyday classroom organisation and routines. Also, remember that any form of assessment which deviates from normal practice is less likely to give a true picture of a child's potential.

Summary records

Again drawing on work undertaken in the two Oxfordshire Schools we are able to suggest the kind of criteria under which brief notes can be made. The frequency with which these 'samples' are compiled is still under review, but once per term seems to be manageable. Each record sheet is headed with the child's name, age and year and the criteria are listed as shown (see Table 5). This format, based on the preceding assessment recommendations, applies to infants *and* juniors by limiting the criteria to those which apply at each key stage.

Assessment of attitudes to reading

Assessment of attitudes is not required by the formal national curriculum assessment procedure. However, for the purposes of planning and monitoring children's developing reading ability, it is essential to take account of their developing attitudes towards books. This kind of information helps teachers to work more effectively with children and provides valuable information for discussion with parents. While such an assessment may well emerge from observations, it is also rewarding to 'interview' children and ask them about their reading.

In individual interviews it is important to ensure that children feel relaxed and confident about their responses. This is helped if teachers *often* spend time talking to children about their reading and about how they feel about it. Teachers can also discuss their own reading with the children and which books they have enjoyed, which they have not and why, explaining about

Date...

Title of Book..

(fiction/non-fiction)

EMERGENT READERS ONLY: NOTES
- plays at reading
- uses book language
- interprets pictures
- focusses on print
  - directionality – front to back
                    – top to bottom
                    – left to right
  - one-to-one correspondence
  - recognises words
  - recognises letters

INDEPENDENT READERS ONLY:
- Use of cues   *Children who are*
  - sound   *reading beyond Level*
  - look   *3 will already be*
  - part of speech   *reading so fluently as*
  - meaning   *to make this part of*
  - pictures   *the record*
- Predicts   *unnecessary.*
- Self corrects
- Refuses
COMPREHENSION:
- recall   *These criteria can be*
- predict outcomes   *applied during a*
- literal   *reading conference by*
- inferential   *asking questions*
- deduction   *about a book read.*
- uses previous experience
TASTES AND PREFERENCES:
- authors   *These criteria can be*
- poets   *applied during a*
- genres   *reading conference*
- home reading   *discussion.*

RETRIEVAL OF INFORMATION:
- knowledge of alphabet   *These criteria can be*
- devises questions   *noted from*
- selects/uses sources   *observation during*
- uses classification system etc.   *project work etc.*
- uses organisational devices.

Table 5

those books which they decided not to finish. Through discussions of this kind children will come to see that they can have control over what and how much they read. Reading is not just a mechanical task of turning and reading all the pages, it is an activity of choice which can be enjoyed. 'Getting lost' in a book should be an ambition of the school reading programme and monitoring the possibility of this happening can take place through an assessment of attitudes towards reading.

The kinds of questions which can be asked are listed below. They can be asked on different occasions so that a review can be made by both teacher and child:

Reading assessment interview

Interview date...Review date....................................
Do you enjoy books?
Which book do you like best?
Why? (Can you tell me about it?)
Do you enjoy listening to stories?
Which story do you like listening to best?
Why? (Can you tell me about it?)
Do you:

- think you are good at reading?
- like to choose your own books?
- like to take books home?
- like to help other children with their reading?
- like other children to help you with your reading?
- like to talk about the books you read?
- like just looking through books?
- like people to read the books you write?

QUESTION

Which other questions would you add to this checklist to reflect the way you organise reading in your classroom?

If you sense that the child's attitude to reading is negative, then use the above checklist to try and identify the specific feature of the activity which they don't like. The interview may well bring to light some facet of that child's reading experience of which you were unaware.

CHAPTER 4

How should reading be developed at Key Stage 1?

What teachers do when they are teaching reading attracts constant attention. This is understandable as people express their concerns about young children, older pupils and adults who find reading difficult. If you are reading this book, it is hard to imagine how different your life might be if you were not able to read accurately, fluently, or even at all. People react to this experience with frustration, anger and sometimes despair.

Observations in schools have led HMI (1990) to describe approaches to teaching reading as one of *mixed methods*, a description which is both accurate and appropriate but misleading. Misleading, because to describe what teachers do as using 'mixed' methods could be misinterpreted. It suggests to some people that teachers are not sure how to approach this part of the English curriculum. It suggests also that teachers change haphazardly between different methods and approaches to the early stage of teaching reading because they are uncertain as to what to do.

This perception of what teachers do is, of course, far from the truth. Marie Clay (1991) has pointed out what children learn from each different approach and, therefore, how no single approach can cover all the teaching and learning which young children need as they progress to become proficient readers. What remains the case is that teachers share a single conception of teaching beginning reading and it is characterised by a variety of teaching activities. This single conception is based on the understanding that young children, born into a print culture, will be learning to read during their pre-school years as well as while they are at school.

All children enter school with some knowledge about written language. This knowledge is dependent on each child's experience of print and varies widely from one child to the next. The skill of the teacher is in knowing the overall thread of development through which all children progress, identifying how far along this line of development an individual child might be on entering school, and then planning programmes of work which ensure that each child continues to make further progress. This is the most successful approach to teaching reading.

Where the misleading perception of *mixed methods* emerges is in relation to what teachers are observed doing in carrying out their teaching plans to meet these individual needs. The single most successful approach in teaching children to read is to provide each child or group of children, through carefully structured experiences, with the most effective and efficient programme which is geared to children's needs and understanding. It is because their needs and understanding change with development, that teachers approach the teaching of reading in different ways with different children or groups of children.

QUESTIONS

What variety of approaches do you use for teaching reading? Do these approaches meet *all* the learning needs of the children in your class?

Developing reading competencies

Observations of young children, both pre-school and during their first two years in school give us a clear idea of the thread of development through which all children make progress. Because this line of development has been identified through observations, it focusses on what children can do at different times as their reading behaviour changes. What is most noticeable from these observations is how children's learning is not a simple straight incremental line of improvement. Children do not just 'get better' at reading in any linear sense.

Reading is a complex activity, requiring the learner to gain control of a number of different skills. These skills are not discrete. They have a relationship with each other, and learning to read also includes gaining control of how the different skills of reading work together to enable the reader to read accurately, fluently and with understanding. In achieving this, the learner is observed to make what can only be described as *progress in fits and starts*. As control of the one set of cues is gained, it appears to be lost for a while when the learner is beginning to interrelate that set with another.

Frequently, learners fail to do on one day what they were well able to do on a previous occasion. Non-professionals working with young children may well find this frustrating and even perverse. However, knowing about this feature of development helps teachers to recognise it as a sign of learning which is characteristic of all complex behaviours. This point is made so that the developmental list which follows is not misunderstood. It is not possible in print to show the recursive nature of learning and a list like this looks like one thing happening after another, which at one level is true. At another level it must be remembered that children's progress through the list of reading competencies shown below happens with much backtracking and leaping ahead. Also this list does not necessarily define a teaching pathway because some children take longer to gain control over certain cue systems whilst other children acquire the different skills almost imperceptibily rapidly.

To help teachers locate a progression of reading development, the different competencies are labelled here with National Curriculum Levels 1–3.

List of developing reading competencies

First Steps (NC Level 1)

(1) Talks about pictures in books.
Asks questions about pictures in books.
Listens to stories and offers to 'read' some.
(2) Makes up own story to print in a picture book.
Uses pictures to cue meaning.
(3) Repeats sentence patterns remembered from texts read aloud.
Self-corrects story retellings using pictures.
Can predict outcomes using pictures.
Cannot identify individual words.

Early Stages (NC Level 1)

(4) Begins to show an interest in printed text.
Asks what the print says.
Can accurately recall stories heard read aloud.
Begins to talk like a book.
(5) Finger and voice pointing, trying to match text.
Asks for unknown words.
Picture cues still important for interpretation of meaning.
Begins to respond to the conventions of text:
   top/bottom of page,
   left/right tracking,
   one page after another.

Beginning Reading (NC Level 2)

(6) Can predict sentence ends.
Begins to understand one-to-one word correspondences.
Begins to identify initial letters of words.
Uses initial letters and pictures to interpret meaning.
(7) Re-reads to make sense of the text.
Reads with word by word voice match.
Uses some graphic cues; initial letters and words endings.

Reading (NC Level 2)

(8) Reads words in known text fluently.
Monitors meaning and self-corrects.
Asks for confirmation of words read.
Semantic and syntactic cues override grapho-phonic cues.
(9) Finds known words in unknown words.
Uses context and grapho-phonic cues.
Reads word by word.
Decoding often inaccurate.

Developing Reading (NC Level 3)

(10) Reads known words and decodes unknown words.
Scans ahead and monitors punctuation.
Uses all available cue systems appropriately.
Reads fluently with expression.
Can read silently.

A list like this (and there are many others) is a composite of a range of observations made by both researchers and teachers (e.g. Clay 1991, Raban, 1984, Waterland, 1988). This list is best used as a means of identifying children's reading behaviour as they enter school and then as a general progress chart to keep track of chidren's development in response to the selected teaching programme. The list also illustrates those points along the route to developing reading where fluency is lost and gained by turn.

ACTIVITY

Look at your own school's developmental checklist against the list printed here. Check that your list identifies the competencies which your children typically exhibit.

First Steps

Being surrounded by print in their lives, young children learn that printed material carries meaning. They learn this through a variety of experiences. For instance:

- adults who look up information in books, lists, catalogues, directories, maps etc.;
- shopping where adults look at labels and parts of the shop are signposted with print, pictures and logos;
- adults responding to posted material, reading newspapers and magazines;
- library visits and bedtime story time.

All these cumulative experiences and many more enable young children to make the connection between what is seen and what is understood.

Children do not start to exercise their own knowledge of this connection between what is seen and what is understood by reading in any technical sense, rather they begin to ask questions about printed material and talk about the pictures they see. Children begin to do what they see others around them doing. A wealth of such evidence is to be found in the tape transcripts of the Bristol Language Development Project. For example, Allan was aged 2 years 3 months when the following conversation took place with his mother as he drank Cherryade at the kitchen table:

> *Allan* And what does that says there?
> *Mother* That's 'Cherryade'.
> *Allan* Look – that's that – same as that, look.
> *Mother* No it isn't. It says 'Family Size'.

And Susan, aged 3 years 3 months, was looking through her mother's hand-bag when she asked:

> *Susan* What does that say?
> *Mother* That's all the list of mummy's addresses.

Also, children imitate reading behaviours, they develop phenomenally precise memories for favourite stories and begin to retell the stories they have heard read aloud, although they cannot identify any individual words at this stage.

QUESTION
How do you identify the knowledge and understanding about print which your children being with them into school?

Early stages

Arising from a rich background of print experiences, children will make progress to this next stage. This shift does not happen by chance – as with all development it needs fostering. The way in which this occurs is by those around the child pointing out words and meanings, taking the child with them to fill the car with petrol, for instance, and showing them how they know to choose the correct nozzle and where it tells them to find air for the tyres or to push the filling station door open. These incidental experiences which we take for granted in our lives, are explicated by parents for their young pre-school children. This kind of repetition in a variety of contexts which constantly makes the match between print and understanding is the all important continuing support for developing reading.

Out of this rich and varied experience, children begin to turn their attention to print they find around them and to ask questions about it. They listen intently to favourite stories read over and over again, being able to accurately recall them and insisting that the reader leaves nothing out. Children will begin to run their fingers along the lines of printed text and say the story they remember. Some words may be recognised, but they will still rely on the picture to feed them with the content of the story.

ACTIVITY

Make a list of the variety of ways in which you can foster children's curiosity about print.

Beginning reading

This Beginning Reading stage is marked by the child's increasing attention to the printed text. Children begin to point out and recognise some of the words and letters with which they are familiar. The letters in their name are particularly salient and naturally are more easily recognised than others. They know from their experience of observing others reading that their own attempts at reading need to make sense. At the beginning of this stage they continue to rely on the pictures for clues to meaning although they are increasingly paying attention to the printed text.

Their apparent early fluency now becomes stilted as they begin to try to match the words they say with the print on the page. By paying attention to the print in this way they notice letters at the beginnings of words and the ways in which words end, although not consistently. They read familiar texts fluently, monitoring the meanings they are making, self-correcting where the meaning puzzles them and asking for confirmation of words they are reading for themselves.

QUESTION

What are the kinds of interventions which teachers can make to support children in monitoring reading while they read? e.g. 'Does it make sense?' 'Go back to the beginning of the sentence.'

Reading

During this stage, children fluctutate between apparently reading known texts fluently, using both syntactic and semantic cues along with the pictures to make the text sensible, and then they appear to read word by word as they begin to pay more attention to grapho-phonemic cues. They can sometimes find known words in unknown words, although their efforts at decoding are frequently inappropriate. When this occurs, they lose their fluency and appear to be at a much earlier stage of development. What is happening here is that the child, while developing a range of cueing systems, cannot yet use them all at once. If one strategy becomes the focus of their reading endeavour, then they lose sight of other strategies. While they know how to make texts make sense, their ability to make their reading accurate is only just beginning to be realised. This is a particularly sensitive time for some children as they can lose confidence if they are not well supported in moving towards accuracy.

QUESTION

How can accuracy in reading be fostered without losing sight of reading for meaning?

Developing reading

Children move into this stage when they are beginning to read both fluently and accurately. They now have sufficient experience of reading and attending to the graphic display, so they can use all available cue systems increasingly efficiently and appropriately. They learn how to decode new words and check their accuracy using meaning and the grammar of their language for confirmation. They scan ahead and anticipate the way the text is progressing and pay attention to punctuation. Children moving through this stage read fluently and with expression.They are confident readers and turn naturally to books for a wide range of purposes.

What children learn from different activities

Hearing stories read aloud

Children who have had stories read or told to them as part of their lives since they were babies will have enjoyed the experience of books thousands of times. Add to this the experience of people around them who point out what print says quite incidentally while enjoying books together, and it becomes clear that these children will arrive in school with a great deal of information about written language. However, being with other people while they do the reading doesn't give young children much of a clue about what to do if they want to read for themselves, except to look at the pages and talk out loud.

Looking at pictures and talking out loud is the characteristic behaviour of a child taking the first steps of reading development. Sensitive teachers build on this experience and continue to share books with children daily. This is the opportunity to begin to draw the children into discussions about the story, the shape of the story, what might happen next and how the picture is an illustration for the text rather than a full record of the story itself. Particularly useful for children at this early stage are books like *Meg and Mog* (Nicoll and Pienkowski 1973) where the print is actually part of the picture. As children memorise the story and look at the pictures for prompts, the print is there for them to see as well, not on another facing page or below the picture.

ACTIVITY

Look again at all the books you use for reading aloud to the children and make a note of the particular features of the reading process which are being developed for the children as they listen.

Big books

In reading stories out loud, big books offer a special opportunity to share the text with a group of children or even the whole class where they can see you pointing to the text as you read to them, inviting them to join in. This sharing of view is essential if you are going to draw children's attention to specific details of how print works:

- reading from top to bottom of pages
- left to right line conventions
- spoken match with each word

Through hearing stories read aloud, children become more familiar with the patterning of written language as opposed to spoken language and this builds up their expectations for when they read themselves. In reading pictures a noticeable development in their reading progress is marked by the way in which they begin to imitate the language of books rather than producing a mere spoken form of response. Children begin to 'talk like a book' as they read the pictures. In discussion, teachers can take the opportunity to focus on particular words to help broaden the children's vocabulary and begin to use some of these new words and different sentence constructions in other classroom activities.

Memorable language patterns

Books which children readily remember and enjoy re-reading for themselves are those which follow a pattern of activity and related language. One example is *Mr Gumpy's Outing* (Burningham 1970) which proceeds page by page with everyone getting into the boat, one page at a time. Inevitably the boat capsizes and the animals each in turn climb out of the water in reverse order. Books of this kind have a satisfying feel to them. Once children know the story they can read it for themselves, using the obvious picture clues. This experience gives children confidence in their first attempts at reading for themselves and helps them to persevere with it.

Other books which are particularly memorable for children include those which have a repeating phrase or sentence pattern. Again, texts like these give children the support they need to read independently. These books not only provide reading aloud material but are also available for the children to read for themselves. In sharing these books with children discussion can include predicting what is coming next, confirming these predictions, helping children to self-correct by showing them what you do to get the reading right. Predicting can start by using a hesitation technique which draws children into the reading:

> Jack and Jill went up the...
> The mouse ran up the...

Asking what is going to happen next before the page is turned, and then confirming what happens by proceeding with the story, gives children a sense of the development of a story and how readers make use of the story up to that point. Readers combine this knowledge of the story so far with experience of the way things are in the real world or world of folk and fairy tales. They do this so that they can make sense of what is going to happen next. By developing this sense of 'what is going to happen next', children gain confidence and fluency in their own retellings.

Books of nursery rhymes which are already known orally provide particularly satisfying reading aloud material as the children will be able to read them for themselves, remembering the pattern of the verse heard so frequently. Reading these aloud will draw children's attention to rhyming words and rhythm in texts which can support the children's growing confidence as they re-read this material for themselves.

Each Peach, Pear Plum (Ahlberg 1978) teaches children to use the pictures to support their predictions. This book draws children into the book by inviting them to use the pictures to engage with the events as they unfold. Further examples of patterning in language at the level of words can be found in the Pat Hutchins' books *The Surprise Party* (Hutchins 1970) and *Don't Forget the Bacon* (Hutchins 1976). These books both entertain and inform the young language user about the way words can be like other words. This is done in the first story through the game of 'chinese whispers' and in the second through a small boy trying to remember his mother's shopping list. Both of these texts lend themselves to follow up activities which are both fun and informative. Activities like saying a word that sounds the same will help to establish the fact that all words are patterned in this way.

Writing

Young children coming into school at five years of age will be just as diverse in their ability to both write and handwrite for themselves as they are in their reading ability. In this book we are not going to directly address either the development of writing or the teaching of writing. However, it is clear that writing has a central role to play in children's developing reading ability and it should be seen as part of the learning-to-read programme. In writing, the child becomes the author *and* the reader. As readers of their own writing they become completely confident readers because they know what the marks on the page say, they know their own intentions in making those marks and can, therefore, share these with others as they read aloud their own stories.

ACTIVITY

Using a large piece of paper or even the blackboard, discuss with the children what is going to be written and write each word for them, talking about the words and letters as the writing takes place. (Writing opportunities like this might be linked to a story read aloud or another experience which all the children have shared.) As each word is written, draw children's attention to how the stream of speech is broken up, leaving spaces between each word.

In constructing their own stories, children need the support of modelling and discussion surrounding the act of writing, just as they have seen reading made explicit during book-share sessions. There will be a place here for making a composite story with a group of children or the whole class joining in each day.

While writing with the whole class in this way, teachers can make use of lists, labels and other printed material around the classroom which gives clues to individual words. An alphabet ordered box of printed *Breakthrough to Literacy* words (Mackay *et al.* 1970) may be a resource which will prove helpful. What the children are experiencing through activities like these is the full range of authoring skills. They are experiencing:

- the connection between having an idea in mind and putting that down on paper;
- the ordered, patterned and conventional means which make print work;
- reinforcement for the conventions of stories;
- print works from top to bottom of the page;
- lines of print go from left to right;
- the stream of speech is being segmented and spaces between words signal this segmentation.

What writing teaches particularly well are the specific features of the graphic display. However, when reading, in order to keep the ideas flowing and retain a level of fluency, attention to the details of individual words and letters will be unhelpful. In writing, it is just these details which will make the print work for a reader. Welding the search for meaning, the quest to make sense of their reading, with the specific features of text which will guide their accuracy, is an important way forward for young children's reading progress. This progress is not gained through any single approach to the teaching of reading, it is forged in the constant reinforcement of all levels of language across a range of literacy activities.

Literacy related activities

Besides actually reading and writing, there will be many other literacy related activities for children. By singing nursery rhymes and alphabet songs, children's attention will be drawn to the beginnings of words, as also by playing 'I Spy . . . ' and other games which might include making displays of objects that begin with the same letter.

ACTIVITY

Children's names are a good starting point for drawing their attention to the beginning of words. Their names can be put in alphabet order by reference to a wall chart, and they can stand in line in alphabet order, rehearsing this when they have to line up at the door. Ask how many letters are represented in the class? How many are not?

Visual and auditory discrimination

> Contrary to popular belief the majority of children are perfectly capable, well before they start school, of making the perceptual discriminations necessary for learning letter shapes.　　　　　　　　Bullock Report 6.15 (DES, 1975)

In view of the large amount of visual perceptual training material which is available for purchase in school catalogues this quotation seems surprising, although on further reflection it is, of course, correct. If children can pick out their carer's face from the crowd at the classroom door, if they can pick up a pin from the floor, their ability to perceive and discriminate between fine differences is well-established. Before learning to read and write children have learned that orientation does not matter in the everyday world of objects and events with which they are most familiar. By this we mean that *b* and *d* are visually distinct pieces of information in reading and writing whilst any other object remains that object even when it is seen turned around the other way. Indeed this is a crucial element of learning that the child has accomplished during the pre-school years, that is, the fact that orientation of objects does not matter.

Conceptual, linked with perceptual conflict, causes extra difficulties of a cognitive nature during these early stages of learning to read whilst children attempt to master the conventions of print. It is not the fact that they can't see the differences between certain letters, rather they don't yet know which differences matter and, therefore, to which differences they should pay attention. For example, the child needs to know that [A] and [a] look different but are the same, [m] and [n] look similar, but are different; that [AND] and [and] look different but are the same, whilst [hat] and [hot] look nearly the same, but are different in an important way. ⸌

These distinctions between what *looks the same or different* and *which differences matter* is best learned by masses of experience of print and by children *seeing* the distinctions that matter *happen before their eyes* in meaningful contexts. This idea is partly what lies behind the often scorned dictum 'Children learn about how to ready by reading', but there is no other way of making such crucial distinctions clear to children. No amount of telling, explaining or drilling will reveal the salience of these distinctions. It is only when children get the distinctions wrong, and it matters, that they will learn to discover that orientation and some fine differences are critical when trying to get the message right, either as a reader or a writer.

Studies have also shown that words which differ markedly from one another
are more easily learned than those between which there is little contrast.
Bullock Report 6.38 (DES, 1975)

It appears, therefore, that training in discrimination activities which do not
involve features of print (how these features will look and how the sounds
become associated with them), will not actually help the child to develop the
kind of discriminatory skill which has been outlined above.

Whilst generalised activities aimed at developing auditory and visual
discrimination will help with learning to read, it is certainly the case that
they do provide teachers with materials, like shape matching and picture
sound matching, which they can use with the children when they first arrive
at school. These materials offer the children activities which enable them to
have time to learn to sit at a table and complete a task; they give children
opportunities to learn how to look after and share materials. The teacher
can observe temperamental characteristics of the children as they attempt
the activity, as well as having a chance to monitor different children's
preferred learning strategies.

QUESTIONS

What sort of discrimination activities do you provide for the children?
What do the children learn from these activities?

Discrimination in the visual field can be helped through games which
involve word matching and pairing, using each child's own sentences,
phrases and word cards, which can also help children to see the differences
and similarities between words. A further stage of letter matching can be
developed from a similar starting point, by taking a well-known word, for
instance the child's name, and cutting the name card at the letter-
boundaries. It is always helpful during these early stages to mark the cards
with a line so that they are easily kept the right way round, for example:

[b] [g] [c]

Familiar games like snap and happy families can form the basis of
reinforcement activities as children become more skilled in their ability to
group these word and letter cards.

Discrimination in the auditory field is developed through nursery rhymes,
jingles and rhyming words. Listening for similarities in sound patterns is
not easy for all children, often they do not know what they are listening for
and miss what we might consider obvious. Well-known rhymes can help
focus their attention on similarities, particularly if the key word is left out
of a rhyming pair for the children to fill in and call out for themselves.

The further ability, to attend to the separate units of sound within words, will be developed through their writing as they begin to use invented spellings based on how they sound the words. To support a whole range of listening skills, games like *Tongue Twisters* can be used to prepare them well for, first *listening* to, then *looking* at the beginnings of words. Later, children's attention can be drawn to the ends of words by making books of repeating sentence patterns:

> I am going fishing
> I am going shopping
> I am going swimming etc..

Sight vocabulary

Building up a sight vocabulary can be very difficult for some children as their concept of a *word* is uncertain. *Word* is not easy to define: for instance the Concise Oxford Dictionary (Sykes, 1976) defines it as:

> any sound or combination of sounds . . . forming a meaningful element of speech . . .   (p. 1343)

Meaningful elements of speech, for young children, are not what we understand as words, they are more often whole phrases or utterances. It is only when we see what the Oxford Dictionary puts in parentheses:

> (or its written or printed symbol, customarily shown with a space on either side of it but not within it)

that we realise the *word* becomes easy to grasp when one can already read and write. For this reason starting reading with *words* using flash cards could present some children with great difficulties of comprehension. To ease this problem we suggest starting with those elements of meaning which the child does respect and understand, that is, the larger unit of the phrase or sentence.

ACTIVITY

At the end of the day's new story, children can match teacher-made cards with their own copies of the appropriate piece of writing, reading them to themselves and going over them with their teacher. Later, the cards could be used for reading independently of the originally written model. After proficiency at this level has been established, and remember that the stock is being added to daily, the sentence cards could be cut at the phrase boundaries so that matching to originals becomes a more complex task (and also more creative) as fresh sentences can be generated by putting different phrases together (i).

(i)

This is my mummy in the garden	sentence card
This is my mummy in the garden	phrase cards
This is my mummy in the garden	phrase cards

We all went to the shops	sentence card
We all went to the shops	phrase cards
We all went in the garden	new sentence

This procedure, when put into practice, involves taking the phrases or sentences which appear in each child's own writing and having them written on a separate card which is kept in the child's writing folder.

Remember that these new sentences as sentence cards and phrase cards have already been recognised and identified on many previous occasions, but this will not necessarily mean that the words on the individual word cards will be automatically recognised in this new form. Once again, the procedure of matching these individual word cards to the sentences from which they are derived will help children to see the connections between sentences and the words which make up those sentences. It will help the children to make this connection if they watch while the cards are cut at the various boundaries. The infinite variety of new sentences which can be generated from these word cards gives another dimension to the reading activities which follow.

This collection of individual word cards for each child will represent a growing 'sight' vocabulary. It is not envisaged that the sequence of events outlined above is separate, but rather they are inter-related activities which continue in parallel as each new stage is developed. It must be emphasised that these activities require a great deal of time and attention. Busy teachers will need the help of parents and older children to provide the instant

(ii)
Cut these cards at the word boundary and work with the children to make completely new sentences.

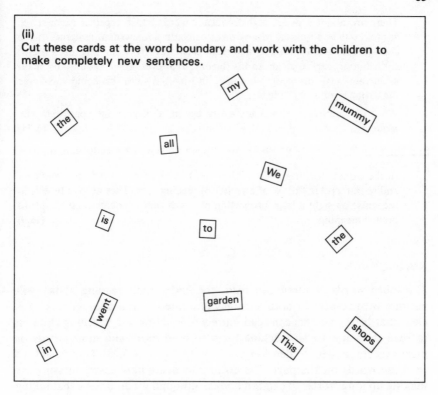

feedback which is necessary for the maintenance of progress. If a child finds some cards too difficult to recognise, then these cards should be put to one side. Remember that children recognise words which are private, personal and picturesque to them. Allow the child, as far as possible, to keep possession of only those cards which *can be read*, so that other games and activities involving the cards can be generated, introducing less well-known words very gradually, leaving them in the context of the known phrase or sentence for as long as necessary before adding them to the word store. Keeping the words in alphabet-ordered pockets can help to reinforce another aspect of learning to read.

QUESTION

What other examples of activities will build up children's sight vocabulary of new words, whilst retaining the context of meaning?

Quotations from the Bullock Report (DES, 1975) lend support to the steps of the procedure we have outlined above:

66

> There are about a dozen high frequency words which together account for
> approximately a quarter of any piece of continuous written material. If the
> child learns these thoroughly and reads them fluently in running text a useful
> contribution can be made to his fluency. However, there should not be an
> undue emphasis on recognising them in isolation since this could encourage
> the wrong kind of learning set. (6.33)
>
> Word recognition is also made easier by the ability to anticipate syntactic
> sequences. (6.34)

and the Cox Report (DES, 1988), amplifies this view of a sight vocabulary:

> In their quest for meaning, children need to be helped to become confident
> and resourceful in the use of a variety of reading cues. They need to be able to
> recognise on sight a large proportion of words they encounter and be able to
> predict meaning. (16.9)

Reading words

The more words children can read, the better their reading ability will
become with respect to both accuracy and fluency. Put another way, it is
clear that better readers can read more words. However, teaching children
to read does not mean teaching them to read more and more words, it
means teaching them to develop as many strategies as possible to be able to
read the words on the page. We do not advocate haphazard guessing, or
making up long stories to caption books, although we do believe that taking
reading *on the run* and risking difficulties (with support and help) will aid
the fluency necessary to get meaning from print. Again the Bullock Report
(DES, 1975) reminds us:

> Word recognition is also made easier by the ability to anticipate syntactic
> sequences. A number of studies show that a printed text is easier to read the
> more closely its structures are related to those used by the reader in normal
> speech.... Research has shown that pre-school children use a surprisingly
> wide range of sentence structures in their spoken language.... Reading
> material which presents children with unreal language therefore lacks
> predictability and prevents them from making use of the sequential
> probability in linguistic structure. (6.34)

Children will use syntactic and semantic cues in word recognition. These are
all basic to language ability and are far more powerful than visual cues
alone. What a word looks like will take a lower level of importance than
what would sound right in context. It is only as the child learns that it
matters to be accurate when one reads, and that such accuracy is achieved
by checking the match between spoken and printed word, that a step
forward is made with reading development. For some children this leap in
understanding happens naturally and quickly, for many others the

misunderstanding of this strategy can hinder their progress and undermine their confidence. Too much reliance on reading the words but not the story, as a teaching strategy, may be adding to this misunderstanding from the child's point of view.

The Cox Report (DES, 1988) points out that:

> Reading is much more than the decoding of black marks on a page: it is a quest for meaning and one which requires the reader to be an active participant. (16.2)

and this view is echoed in further guidance (NCC 1989) for implementing the National Curriculum:

> When we read something we *make* sense of it for ourselves, not just by 'decoding' but by bringing our own experience and understanding to it. (6.1)

Books for children at this stage of development should provide the necessary experiences to help them to gather momentum in their reading ability after their first steps in reading have been taken. The books will not necessarily increase in reading difficulty, but they will increase in other respects. The books get longer, there is more print on each page, there is less reliance on picture cues, books of different types and styles all provide for the wide range of reading which will help the children's reading ability to develop. The range of vocabulary and syntactic structures begins to increase and allows the children to make greater use of their knowledge of language. Children should experience development of their understanding of reading in terms of what it is for and how one does it, by reading widely throughout these early stages.

Using syntactic and semantic cues

In the following sentence: *Jup is settling down the wugmup*, it is easy to recognise straight away that *settling* is a verb and *Jup* and *wugmup* are nouns. It is in the nature of word strings that they identify the grammatical function of each word. The grammar of a sentence is related to the meaning it conveys and it is our tacit grammatical sense which helps us to understand what we hear and read. The ability to handle language sequences of this kind is referred to in the Bullock Report (DES, 1975), where it is stated (6.34) that word recognition is made easier by the ability to anticipate syntactic sequences. If we look at the sentence: 'John had a lot of work to do so he . . . ' you can say with conviction that the next word is likely to be a verb and this ability instantly reduces the possibilities from which to choose, rather than expecting *any* word in the English language to follow. Clearly, this ability is extremely useful as:

> words are recognised as a result of matching a small number of possibilities

against the printed model rather than by mechanically working through all the possible sound values of the separate elements.

Bullock Report 6.31 (DES, 1975)

QUESTIONS

How then, are children to use these skills in their reading; skills they readily use in the context of oral language? How do you develop this aspect of children's knowledge about language and help them to develop explicit understanding about how to make use of semantic and syntactic strategies?

Knowledge about language

Many teachers make use of a word bank of some kind; probably the most popular is the *Breakthrough Sentence Maker* (Mackay B. *et al.* 1970) or a home-made version of something similar. Look carefully to see how these words are arranged in the folder. Some are likely to be in alphabetical order, which makes sense for *us*, but how much sense does this make for *children*? Consider the situation of a child wanting to construct a sentence from the words in the word folder. If the words are grouped together by their initial letter, then it is expected that the child will begin to understand

---

ACTIVITY
A simple form of this material could be made on large cards for the use of groups of children, and a wall-mounted container made to keep the cards in their respective sections.

blue	red	green
John	is	big
Pat	will be	cross
The dog	has been	ill

blue	red	green
The boy	has been	naughty

the systematic relationship between these particular correspondences. Alongside this, it might be worth thinking of a different type of organisation of the words in these folders, bearing in mind what has been said earlier. Another way of organising the words could be to use different coloured cards for the different parts of speech (if you make your own word banks); otherwise marking the cards in some way with a coloured line to indicate nouns, verbs, etc. Words and/or phrases could be used and games might help the children to gain some insight into sentence structures.

This material could take the alternative form of words on each face of a roller, with each roller being made of differently coloured card containing other pertinent sentences about different children. With either arrangement, multiple combinations can be made to the great delight of the children. Remember to include yourself – 'my teacher is happy', 'our teacher is tired'!

ACTIVITY

A way of using this material could be based on the techniques of *cloze procedure*, where sentences are constructed with one word missed out. Which colour cards are most likely to fill the gap? Having alerted the children to this strategy of selecting the appropriate colour cards from the word bank, then they can try out various possibilities which will all fit.

Some of the results of this activity may well be very funny and this is usually highly motivating for the children. If the wrong colour cards are selected for fitting in the gap, then the sentences just won't work at all. So the pay-off is seen as going for the right part of speech each time – even though the children will not be explicitly aware of overt sentence parsing.

ACTIVITY

As a preparation to activities like this, gather a group of children round in a circle and ask one of them to start a sentence by saying the first word. They can't just say any word, it must be one that starts a sentence, for example; *I, The, Once, How*. Each child takes a turn to follow on with one more word until the sentence is complete and then they can start again.

Some children find this activity great fun, although there may be others who find it very bewildering. It is usually easier to start the sentence off than to try and follow someone else's lead, so those who have some difficulty should be encouraged to think of a starting word and then listen to the others until they feel they can join in later.

ACTIVITY

The above activity can be followed by the teacher writing down the word each child says on an appropriately coloured card which they hold, and after the sentence has been completed the cards can be read by the other children, before they have a turn in following each other with a word.

These games and activities help children to see that something *they already know and can do* gives them a chance to have a go at something they can't yet do quite so well – read.

Phonics: how and when?

The debate as to whether or not to include phonics in a learning-to-read programme was also dealt with by the Bullock Report (DES, 1975):

> Competence in phonics is essential both for attacking unfamiliar words and for fluent reading. The question, then, is not whether or not to teach phonics; *of this there is no doubt.* The question is how and when to do it. (6.23)

It is clear that phonics is easy when you can read. This may sound trite but consider it further. An example of what is meant here is illustrated in the Bullock Report (DES, 1975):.

> The word printed below gives some impression of the kind of problem that confronts a child when he has to combine graphemes (the ink marks on the page) with phonemes (the sounds of spoken language) in a phonic attack on an unfamiliar word: *colmbost.* (6.20)

The word *colmbost* is difficult to read although the letters represent sounds they often stand for. Children, during the early stages of learning to read, will not know the rules which govern sound-symbol correspondences, neither explicitly nor at an intuitive level. Even knowing these rules may not always help, as sound-symbol permutations are so numerous. Children can learn these correspondences in one of two ways: by having their attention deliberately drawn to the letters, their sounds and the ways in which both are related, or by discerning these correspondences visually from their experience of print. All teachers come across children who have acquired phonic knowledge intuitively. The question remains as to how we are to help those children who need more assistance than others in making these phonic generalisations.

Returning to the original point that phonics is probably easier when you can read, the Bullock Report (DES, 1975) continues by saying:

> Our analysis of the problem has led us to the view that it is better for children to learn phoneme-grapheme relations in the context of whole word recognition, at least in the early stages of reading. (6.26)

This suggests that children will be better able to learn phonic possibilities when these are demonstrated for them using words they can already recognise to illustrate the point. Before children have a vocabulary of sight words, they will find phonic analysis and synthesis far too abstract to be of any use in learning to read unfamiliar words. This does not mean that they should not be introduced to the concept of letters and the sound patterns of the language. These factors are obviously essential elements in the early stages of a child's understanding of printed and spoken language (and their intricate interdependence) and should be beginning to develop as they make progress with their reading. The Cox Report (DES, 1988) picks up this theme in stressing that children need:

> ...to be able to predict meaning on the basis of phonic, idiomatic and grammatical regularities and of what makes sense in context... (16.9)

There is ample evidence to reassure us that phonics is an appropriate strategy for children to use in their efforts to master print, although we are clearly alerted to its dangers if too simply conceived and there are other equally important strategies which should also be included in any learning to read programme. It also seems to be the case that a pre-phonic phase would help many children over this difficult stage. For example, rhyming word games can be played at the level of spoken language long before these assocations are made with print.

QUESTIONS

What are we hoping to achieve with any particular child? What are the best ways of getting there? A little later ask: Are we succeeding? [If not, then review the appropriate emphasis for a particular child across the range of possible cue systems and adjust your own support for that child accordingly.]

Phonics and Reading

Research evidence suggests that children who are good readers make use of phonic knowledge and yet there is also evidence which indicates that teaching phonic skills to children in the early stages of reading will not necessarily improve reading ability. Children do need the opportunity for learning phonic generalisations. However, this is not necessarily achieved by teaching phonics as a separate set of skills, more often this learning is accomplished by providing children with appropriate experiences of reading texts and heightening sensitivity to the patterns in language.

Instructing children in phonic skills will not of itself ensure that they master them. Listening to children read aloud provides a rich source of information concerning the ways in which they tackle print, revealed through the inaccuracies or mistakes that they make. An analysis of these quickly shows two important cues that children respond to: *the letter at the beginning of the word and the length of the word*. It therefore remains important that children learn to make use of this source of information, although teaching children the sounds of the letters out of context may not be the most appropriate way of ensuring that this occurs.

From the Bullock Report (DES, 1975):

> What we criticise is the unsubtle practice of encouraging children to build up words by *sounding* letters as a routine practice. (7.24)

We all know that children will learn more easily with material that is both motivating and meaningful, and because of this it must be inappropriate to introduce phonic work right at the start of formal reading instruction. The whole notion of phonics is conceptually abstract and very probably uninteresting for beginning readers, so it is best to let them develop some reading skills initially, for example by reading captions and sentences which have been written to their dictation. The Cox Report (DES, 1988) points out that:

> Teachers should recognise that reading is a complex but unitary process and not a set of discrete skills which can be taught separately in turn and, ultimately, bolted together. (16.9)

During the early stages children will find helpful games which focus their attention on the beginnings of words. Material from the *Words and Pictures* BBC Schools Television Teachers' Notes contain many examples of this kind of work.

QUESTION

Can you think of other activities which will develop children's early phonic skills?

ACTIVITY

One game involves selecting two or three letter cards and placing these on the table where a group of children can see them. Call a word and the children point to the letter it begins with.

ACTIVITY
Make up sheets for the children to find the pictures which begin like the picture in the middle of the page. They can draw a circle round those pictures which begin in the same way.

Visual phonics

Building up a personal collection of sight words, described earlier in this chapter, also provides the basis for early phonic work. Words which children can read on sight will be available from their own work and from the early reading books they will be enjoying. The beginning letter of each of these words can be copied onto separate cards and used by the children to match with the words they can read.

This game can be played without the teacher; all that is required is a pile of word cards which the children can read, and their associated initial letter cards. Each child takes it in turn to call a word and confirm that the group's response is correct. Some timid and diffident children find it more helpful to join in a group like this as they feel safer copying what the others do for a while before they risk their own responses. Looking closely at the individual sight vocabulary built up for each child, it will not be surprising to discover that many words are the same for the group as a whole. For instance, *am, at, an, up,* may well be among them. Use these as the basis for the next stage of the phonic programme where one is trying to give the children some insight into the structure of words.

ACTIVITY

Place letter cards in front of the words already selected, like the examples give above: *at* becomes *mat, bat, hat, rat, fat, cat,* etc., and the children call out each new word as it is made. Different kinds of apparatus can make this stage fun for the children:

- a collar on an empty kitchen roll
- a card strip and a window
- separate cards

Also use the separate letter cards to help children listen for the *ends of words*. To do this, use short words as before and, after placing two or three letter cards on the table, ask the children to point to the letter at the end of the word called.

Children listen very hard during this activity, saying the word for themselves over and over until finally they can segment the discrete units of sound, isolating the last sound and subsequently identifying it from the alternatives displayed. If you can get your children this far without ever telling them the *sounds* of the letters then they really must have taught themselves, and the skill will therefore mean more to them.

Remember that introducing children to the separate sounds of the letters may not be the best way of beginning phonic work. Rather, *listening* to the sounds in words and looking at the letters, what is called here 'visual phonics', will provide a firmer base for encouraging children to use phonic cues in their reading of continuous text.

> Broadly speaking there are two ways in which a child can learn the correspondences between phonemes and graphemes. One is by attending directly to the sounds and letters and the way they relate to one another. The other is by attending to whole words and their pronunciation, and over a period of time learning to make intuitive generalisations about phoneme-grapheme relationships.   Bullock Report 6.23 (DES, 1975)

Reading unknown words

A common difficulty for children reading aloud at this level is that of the 'look and guess' technique which some children adopt when they meet unfamiliar words. This strategy fails to provide them with ways of checking the accuracy of their predictions. One of the more obvious cue levels often chosen for explicit teaching is that of sound/symbol correspondence. As suggested before, most children make adequate use of cues at the level of syntax but sometimes come to rely on these alone. They read so inaccurately as to obscure the meaning of the text altogether and consequently they cannot make use of expectations at the semantic level and cannot then self-correct. The mature reader uses many cue levels when reading fluently, therefore it would be a mistake to over-emphasise one skill at the risk of children no longer using other strategies. Sole emphasis on the 'phonic' approach is a case in point.

It cannot be stressed often enough that successful reading depends on the reader having a flexible approach to features of the text. If children have only one way of looking at print they are unlikely to make progress and become successful readers. Because of this, books may well become a source of frustration to some children and one way of dealing with this issue is reading the text to them without any obligation for they themselves to read aloud. This paves the way towards a more relaxed attitude towards books. Easing children towards books in this way will set the scene for more intensive work on the skills and strategies needed for further progress.

Programme of Study for Key Stage 1

Paragraph 7 of the Programme of Study (DES/WO 1990) summarises what is required in the teaching of reading for children at Key Stage 1:

> Pupils should be taught to–
>> ● appreciate the significance of print and the fact that pictures and other visual media can also convey meaning, e.g. *road signs, logos*;

- build up, in the context of their reading, a vocabulary of words recognised on sight;
- use the available cues, such as pictures, context, phonic cues, word shapes and the meaning of a passage to decipher new words;
- be ready to make informed guesses, and to correct themselves in the light of additional information, e.g. *by reading ahead or looking back in the text*;
- develop the capacity to convey, when reading aloud, the meaning of the text clearly to the listener through the intonation and phrasing;
- develop the habit of silent reading. (para 7)

These six points cover the broad base of a teaching reading programme and provide a valuable checklist for planning in development and evaluating schemes of work.

CHAPTER 5

How should reading be developed at Key Stage 2?

The pen-portrait of an upper-junior class in Chapter One included a number of issues which deserve detailed examination. In particular HMI have, in recent years, highlighted two areas of reading development which require further attention in the junior years:

- Reponse to literature
- Information retrieval

These two issues will be discussed in turn.

Response to literature

> Once a week the children come in from play, take a book from their trays and arrange themselves into groups of four. For fifteen minutes they tell each other about the book they've enjoyed most since last week, selecting an appetite-whetting extract to read aloud in such a way as to interest the other children in the book.
> (Year 4 Teacher)

This 'sharing' of books (we call it a bookshare session) is valuable for many reasons but principally because book recommendations are more powerful if they are:

- spoken rather than written
- child-to-child rather than teacher-to-child

A simple activity like this can operate successfully throughout the primary school but can be developed further once the children are fluent readers.

Recent HMI reports have been critical of approaches to fiction and poetry in the later junior years:

> With regard to the study of literature in Year 6, the work in general was not determined by a clear or coherent policy for literature.
> (DES/WO, 1989a, Para 19)

At the start of the last year in Key Stage 2 the pattern of teaching mirrored that emerging at Year 3. The majority of children, having achieved at least a satisfactory level of fluency, had left the reading programme to be 'free readers'. Most of their reading experience was from books which they selected from class libraries, read on their own in school and at home, and sometimes evaluated in the form of books reviews or diaries. The teacher monitored the children's reading, but too infrequently discussed books with them and for the majority, reading was individual and inadequate guidance was given on which books to read. (HMI, 1990, para. 52)

The Cox Report provides a considered rationale for developing response to literature of all kinds in the primary years. They refer to 'active involvement' and the fostering of empathy through 'vicariously entering the worlds of others' (DES/WO, 1986, p. 27). A further justification given is the understanding of allusions to literature in the cultural heritage of the English-speaking world. These concerns are encapsulated in a clear strand of 'response' criteria in Statements of Attainment such as:

Level 1. Talk in simple terms about the content of stories....
Level 2. Listen and respond to stories, poems and other material read aloud, expressing opinions informed by what has been read.
Level 3. Listen attentively to stories, talk about setting, story-line and characters and recall significant details.
Level 4. Demonstrate, in talking about a range of stories and poems which they have read, an ability to explore preferences.
Level 5. Demonstrate, in talking or writing about fiction, poetry, non-fiction and other texts that they are developing their own views and can support them by reference to some details in the text.

(DES/WO, 1990, pp. 7–9)

The Programme of Study for Key Stage 2 states that pupils should:

... be encouraged to respond to the plot, character or ideas in stories or poems, and to refer to relevant passages or episodes to support their opinions. (DES/WO, 1990, p. 31)

Non-Statutory Guidance (NCC 1990) contains quite explicit recommendations and examples (Section D1–D5) including suggested activities under five headings:

- plot
- characters
- setting
- theme
- style and genre.

Certainly a 'clear and coherent policy for literature' at Key Stage 2 can be formulated by reference to National Curriculum documents along with advice gleaned from other sources. Two useful starting points are Somerfield *et al.* (1983, Chapter Seven 'Introducing Children to Literature') and Dougill and Knott (1988, Chapter Four 'Reading for meaning, for pleasure and for life'). Trevor Cairney (1990, pp. 53–68) describes nine strategies for 'developing the comprehension of literary texts' and these are briefly summarised below:

(1) COLLABORATIVE STORIES
   – using no-text versions of picture books
(2) TEXT SHUFFLE
   – sequencing a scrambled version of a text
(3) STORY FRAMES
   – providing a framework for recall of a story
(4) STORY TRANSFORMATION
   – children present story (with props) to others
(5) CHARACTER MUG SHEETS
   – providing a framework for summaries of character's appearance/traits etc.
(6) WRITTEN CONVERSATION WITH A CHARACTER
   – children imagine and record their conversations with a book character
(7) NEVER-ENDING STORY
   – providing the start of a story which is then continued by each child in turn
(8) CHARACTER INTERVIEWS
   – children interview a story character
(9) LITERARY SOCIOGRAM
   – children draw a diagram showing the connections between characters in a story

A key text for teachers of upper juniors is undoubtedly that of Michael Benton and Geoff Fox (1985). This covers all genres from picture books to poetry and novels suitable for different ages and includes valuable 'teaching sequences' and 'teaching ideas' throughout. There are 'ten things schools could do' (pp. 99–100) and details of 18 activities centred on a class novel (pp. 127–131), all of which can be adapted to the serialised reading aloud of a story with classes throughout the junior school. In a separate chapter entitled 'Teaching Poems' Benton and Fox suggest various ways of introducing poetry and provide seven examples of starting points for individual reflection (pp. 142–4) followed by 13 group/class activities designed for 'sharing, modifying and development of individual responses.' (pp. 147–9).

We certainly consider that Benton and Fox provide the most

comprehensive and practical guide to developing response to literature in the junior years. Gwen Gawith (1990) clearly builds on their work in her collection of copyright-free A4 worksheets which progress beyond her earlier work on reading report forms (Gawith, 1988). In the later collection she is aiming at the 8–14 age range and intends that the activities should:

> ...make it easier for children to share and extend their feelings and opinions about books; to provide a focus for their discussions.   (Gawith, 1990, p. 10)

Example 1 demonstrates how Gawith's resources can be further enhanced by inviting children to *design their own* reading response forms. The children involved were a mixed class of Years 5 and 6. They were introduced to the *Reading is Feeling* activity (Gawith, 1990, p. 41) which is reproduced here by kind permission of A. & C. Black.

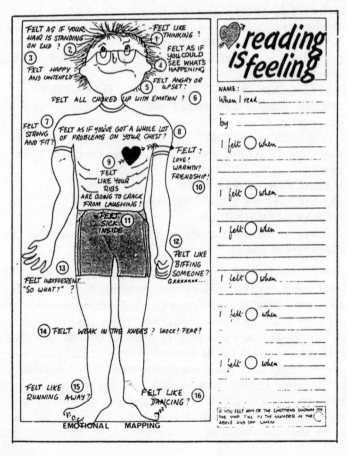

Example 1

The children then had to think of a story they had recently read and complete brief details about parts of the story which engendered different feelings. The children later discussed the activity and their forms were displayed in the library corner for others to share. The following week the same children were invited to design their own forms and others in the class opted for the one they would like to complete. Examples 2 and 3 demonstrate the outcome.

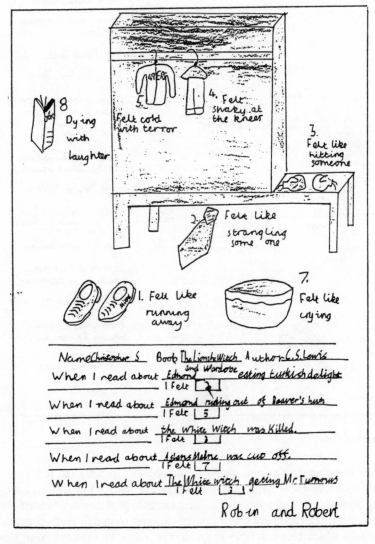

Example 2

82

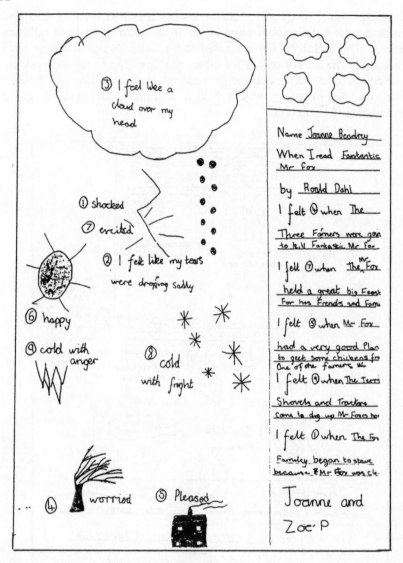

Example 3

The 'Reading is Feeling' activity focusses on emotional response to literature whilst other aspects of reflection are fostered in different ways. Gwen Gawith's *zodiaction* (p. 47), for example, provides resumés of signs of the zodiac characteristics and invites children to match story characters to the sign which best describes them. In the following example Aunt Cress was unanimously designated 'virgo' because:

She brings her own rubber gloves and bleach and off she goes, whacking bleachy water in the sinks and down the loo and along the skirting-boards and on the door handles . . .   (Whybrow, 1989, p. 11)

Gawith's description of a virgo is 'conscientious, likes perfection . . . likes efficiency, seeks order.' Aunt Cress is a character in the *The Sniff Stories* by Ian Whybrow and the matching of Dad, Mum, Ben, Sal and Aunt Cress to zodiac sings was *one* of the activities of a class of juniors engaged in after the teacher had read aloud the first story, 'Enter Sniff'. But first the children were engaged in group reflection and response:

(1)   The teacher read the first three pages which introduce the family, but not Sniff.
(2)   Pairs of children were asked to consider and comment upon:
 • what the house was like
 • what mum, dad, Ben and Sal were like
 • who/what Sniff might be.
(3)   The next seven pages were read aloud. These deal with Ben and Sal finding Sniff in the playground. Sniff is a harum-scarum kind of dog and he is taken home just as preparations are being made to welcome the fastidious Aunt Cress. We have also been introduced to the way Sal speaks, ('I dot a doggie')
(4)   The next page of the story was then given to pairs of children to complete. All direct speech had been removed (see examples).
(5)   Predictions were compared with the original text and the story was read to the end.

This activity took well over an hour to complete and led to some intensive discussions within and between pairs of children. The teacher had recently introduced work on direct and indirect speech so the completion task was partly a consolidation of that work. The children also had to bear in mind the way toddler Sal spoke and, at the bottom of the example reproduced here (Example 4), you can see that Caroline and Becky were aware of the effect a dog like Sniff might have on Aunt Cress.

QUESTION

What else were the children learning from this activity?

One of the activities suggested by Benton & Fox is:

writing extracts from different characters' diaries which might include their guesses about what might happen, their plans, their opinions of other characters, as well as accounts and appraisals of things past.

(Benton & Fox, 1985, p. 125)

‘ ,’ Sal yelled above the noise of the machine. The dog tugged itself out of her clasp and attacked the Hoover, pushing at the brush with his front paws together and biting energetically at the bag. When Dad turned the machine off (which he did with great speed) the dog lay and looked at it hopefully, waiting for it to roar again.

‘ ?’ he said.

‘ ,’ said Sal. ‘ .’

By now Mum had arrived. The dog jumped up and pushed its wet nose into her apron.

‘ ,’ explained Sal.

‘ ,’ said Mum. She didn’t really know whether to be embarrassed at the amount of sniffing going on or to be pleased by the affection she was getting.

‘ ’ said Sal. ‘ .’

‘ ?’ my dad asked me.

‘ ,’ I said. ‘ .’

‘ ,’ said Sal. ‘ .’

‘ ?’ said Mum. ‘ ?’

‘ ,’ said Sal. ‘ .’

Caroline & Becky

‘look dat I dat ,’ Sal yelled above the noise of the machine. The dog tugged itself out of her clasp and attacked the Hoover, pushing at the brush with his front paws together and biting energetically at the bag. When Dad turned the machine off (which he did with great speed) the dog lay and looked at it hopefully, waiting for it to roar again.

‘Whats that ?’ he said.

‘Its a doddy ,’ said Sal. ‘all nice and’ fluffy

By now Mum had arrived. The dog jumped up and pushed its wet nose into her apron.

‘I found da doddy ad da park,’ explained Sal.

‘Oh really I wonder what its sniffing at,’ said Mum. She didn’t really know whether to be embarrassed at the amount of sniffing going on or to be pleased by the affection she was getting.

‘Me want keep doddy’ said Sal. ‘Its all hairy .’

‘Did you really think we were going to keep it?’ my dad asked me.

‘Just for 1 night,’ I said. ‘it wont be any trouble .’

‘nice doddy,’ said Sal. ‘Me want keep .’

‘I wonder what the food would cost?’ said Mum. ‘I suppose you could kee it as long as you keep it out the way But I wonder what Aunt cress will say ?’

‘Ypee,’ said Sal. ‘Me keep doddy’

These pages are reproduced hy kind permission of Random House Century Publishers.

Example 4

The following format (Example 5), enlarged to A4 size, is a useful starting point although some stories/characters might lend themselves to more extended journal or log entries rather than this ‘week-at-a-glance’ approach.

These examples of activities undertaken in junior schools serve to merely illustrate ways in which children can be encouraged to reflect upon and respond to literature which they read individually or have read aloud to them. As we said earlier they are only indicative of the wealth of ideas suggested by Benton & Fox (1985), Gawith (1990), Cairney (1990) and Non-Statutory Guidance (NCC 1990). These four sources could well form the basis of the ‘clear and coherent policy’ advocated by HMI. Even then there will be unexpected events which offer additional ideas and opportunities. When Roald Dahl died in November 1990, extracts from newspaper obituaries were read to a class of top juniors and the children were asked if they would like to draft their own obituaries. Their contributions are part accolade, part critical review but, more than that, the teacher’s invitation

```
PRINT YOUR NAME HERE _____

A week in the life of _____ who appears in the book _____

                                              by _____

MONTH _____ YEAR _____
```

Monday	Thursday
Tuesday	Friday
Wednesday	Saturday
	Sunday

Example 5

gave them the chance to reflect on their deeply personal relationship with a writer who had been party to their emotional and literary growth . . .

'I am sad because I wondered if he was going to write a new book.
My mum thinks he's a bit nasty and funny.
I like how he makes it sound real.'

'I have not outgrown his books at all.
I still think them very funny.
I started reading them when I was 6 or 7 years old.'

'I liked his books when I was 8 and I think I have outgrown him now.'

'Roald Dahl was a famous writer.
He was not my favourite writer but he wrote a lot of children's books.'

'I think that *James and the Giant Peach* and *George's Marvellous Medicine* are the best because they've got humour and something serious.'

'Some of the things Roald Dahl writes other authors wouldn't dream of writing.'

'I think his books were popular because he kind of thought like a child.'

'I think his books have everything a book needs – adventure, humour, sad part, happy part.'

'I enjoyed most of his books but every now and again he slipped up.'

'I didn't really take to Roald Dahl...'

An extremely useful file of annotations of 332 books suitable for upper juniors has been produced by Harcourt Brace Janovich Ltd: *Hooked on Books* (1990). It covers novels, picture books, collection of short stories, books in series, 42 subject indexes and photocopiable booklists for parents. This resource will certainly save time as well as providing information about a range of books for 9–11 year olds.

Poetry

A wealth of advice and practical suggestions for developing response to poetry as well as guidance on children writing poetry can be found in the following selection of books for teachers:

Balaam, J. & Merrick, B.	*Exploring Poetry 5–8*, NATE, 1987
Brownjohn, Sandy	*Does it have to Rhyme?*, Hodder & Stoughton, 1980
Brownjohn, Sandy	*The Ability to Name Cats*, Hodder & Stoughton, 1989
Brownjohn, Sandy	*What Rhymes with Secret?*, Hodder & Stoughton, 1982
Cook, Helen & Styles, Morag	*There's a Poet Behind You*, A.& C. Black, 1988
Corbett, Pie & Moses, Brian	*Catapults and Kingfishers: Teaching Poetry in Primary Schools*, O.U.P., 1986
Hughes, Ted	*Poetry in the Making*, Faber, 1967
Pirrie, Jill	*On Common Ground: A programme for teaching poetry*, Hodder & Stoughton, 1987
Styles, Morag & Dunn, J.	*In Tune with Yourself*, C.U.P., 1987
Styles, Morag & Triggs, Pat	*Poetry 0–16, Books for Keeps*, 1988

Michael Jones compiles Kaleidoscope Poetry Boxes for Infant and Junior age children and his teachers' notes contain 25 different classroom activities centred on poetry. These are available from *Books for Students*, Warwick (See Chapter Seven).

Plays

Several series of plays for group reading are available and these offer two possibilities:

- reader support in a group
- group discussion/response arising from the play

A recommended selection follows:

> *Playmakers* (C.U.P.)
> *Storychest* (Nelson) Two plays in each stage
> *Sunshine Books* (Heinemann)
> *Take Part* and *Take Part Starters* (Ward Lock)

A variety of ways to develop group reading and exploration of literature are provided in Bentley and Rowe (1991). This inexpensive booklet also includes a useful introduction to reader response theory as well as examples of 'Story Maps and Shapes' and 'Literary Sociograms'.

Information Retrieval

> We have been failing to point out to our young readers that in order to gain information from project books, the reader must read the books with a different reading strategy from that used when reading fiction.
>
> (Neate, 1988, p. 42)

The National Curriculum has a good deal to say about information retrieval or *reading for learning* as it is often called. Originally the strand of statements embedded in the Reading Attainment Target were organised as a separate AT with a 30% weighting within the Reading PC (DES/WO, 1988b) but the consultation exercise revealed overwhelming opposition to this and when the second Cox Report was published (DES/WO, 1989a), the two ATs were conflated and have remained so ever since. However the strand is easily identified within each level:

Level 1. Talk in simple terms about the content of stories, or information in non-fiction books.

Level 2. Read accurately and understand straightforward signs, labels and notices.
Demonstrate knowledge of the alphabet in using word books and simple dictionaries.

Level 3. Devise a clear set of questions that will enable them to select and use appropriate information sources and reference books from the class and school library.

Level 4. Demonstrate, in talking about stories, poems, non-fiction and other texts, that they are developing their abilities to use inference, deduction and previous reading experience.
Find books or magazines in the class or school library by using the classification system, catalogues or database and use appropriate methods of finding information, when pursuing a line of enquiry.

Level 5. Demonstrate, in talking or writing about fiction, poetry, non-fiction and other texts that they are developing their own views and can support them by reference to some details in the text.

Select reference books and other information materials and use organisational devices to find answers to their questions and those of others.

(DES/WO, 1990)

These statements contain clues as to the intentions which underlie them. There is, for example, an emphasis on *talking* about what is being learnt from information books. The learning of library reference skills is not seen as a discrete set of skill-learning exercises because of the carefully positioned phrase 'when pursuing a line of enquiry.' It is also assumed that primary schools will have libraries and that those in junior departments/schools will have classification systems and catalogues.

QUESTION

What else can you infer from the Statements of Attainment reproduced above?

The Programmes of Study amplify these intentions, first for Key Stage 1 by describing the learning environment:

Pupils should encounter an environment in which they are surrounded by books and other reading material presented in an attractive and inviting way. The reading material should include material which relates to the real world, such as labels, captions, notices, children's newspapers, books of instructions, plans and maps, diagrams, computer printout and visual display.

(DES/WO, 1990, p. 29)

Then, in detailing children's entitlement:

Activities should ensure that pupils:

refer to information books, dictionaries, word books or simple data on computers as a matter of course. Pupils should be encouraged to formulate first the questions they need to answer by using such sources, so that they use them effectively and do not simply copy verbatim.

... talk about the content of information books.   (DES/WO, 1990, p. 30)

Additionally, at Key Stage 2 ...

Pupils should:

... be shown how to read different kinds of materials in different ways, e.g. 'search' reading to find a scientific or geographical fact;

... learn how to find information in books and databases, sometimes drawing on more than one source, and how to pursue an independent line of enquiry.

And specifically for children working towards Level 5:

Pupils should be taught how to interpret and use organisational devices such as chapter titles and headings, subheadings, changes in print or typeface, and keys to symbols to abbreviations. (DES/WO, 1990, p. 31)

So far the emphasis has been upon the *skills* which children should be developing in order to meet the criteria set out at each level but Non-Statutory Guidance at Key Stage 2 is much more concerned with the *process* of learning:

> At KS2 children need to know how to find information, and be aware that information books need *not* be tackled as a complete 'read' starting at page 1.
>
> ... In making use of reference materials, children will resort to copying the text unless the task they are undertaking requires interpretation of what has been read. They will need activities which lead them to formulate their own questions, identify main points and gather relevant evidence from a number of sources. (NCC, 1990, B5)

Indeed it is this process which HMI highlighted in a report which was very critical of the reading-for-learning competence of top juniors:

> The threefold process of forming appropriate questions, selecting and reading texts to find information and writing it up in their own words had not been taught to or acquired by many pupils. (DES/WO, 1989a, p. 6)

Skills

By clearly contextualising reading-for-learning skills in 'enquiry' or 'project' work, the National Curriculum is in line with authorities like Sarah Tann (1988) and David Wray (1985 and 1988) who, when talking for example about alphabetical order, mentions young children who 'pick up the skill by using encyclopaedias or dictionaries to find out more about subjects which interest them.' (Wray, 1988, p. 12). One of the best ways to learn reference skills is to be personally involved with them.

ACTIVITY

Consider the following activities and see if you can extend/develop them:

- Children construct their own personal dictionaries of the words they are familiar with/use in their writing. They, not teachers, head up each page with the letter of the alphabet. When asking for a word, they attempt to have their dictionary open at the appropriate page.
- When using a published dictionary they try opening it as near as possible to the letter they require (e.g. E near the beginning, T near the end). *Continued*

ACTIVITY *Continued*

• Even the simplest books made by children can contain an index. A six-page book about 'My Dog' might have an index like:

  Food   Page 4
  Sleep   Page 2
  Walk   Page 5

Children are then engaged in two important skills:

(1) Identifying main ideas.
(2) Alphabetical order.

Both Sarah Tann and David Wray provide lists of the skills which are involved in information retrieval:

- identifying the information
- selecting possible sources
- locating the information
- extracting and recording the information
- interpreting/integrating/interrogating information
- presenting findings   (Tann, 1988, pp. 33–34)

Wray draws on the classifications set out by Winkworth (1977) and discusses each in turn:

- define subject and purpose
- locate information
- select information
- organise information
- evaluate information
- communicate results   (Wray, 1985, pp, 13–17 Wray, 1988, pp. 16–18)

A simpler classification, drawn from the Schools Council 'Reading for Learning' projects (Lunzer & Gardner, 1979 and 1984) and subsuming the steps listed above, is represented by the mnemonic LOR:-

  L ocate   ⎫
  O rganise   ⎬ information
  R econstruct   ⎭

Various ways to help children learn these skills and processes have been documented by Lunzer and Gardner but almost exclusively with reference to secondary-age children where the project was targeted. The implications for primary children are far-reaching and will be discussed in some detail but first, two further examples of activities which are firmly directed by the teacher but which occur within the context of on-going project work and help to steer children away from verbatim copying:

ACTIVITY 1: *(for younger/less fluent readers)*

(1) Choose an information book from our project collection on 'food'.
(2) Make sure it is a book you can read.
(3) Read a few pages until you have found out something you did not already know.
(4) Close the book.
(5) Write about the thing you found out and draw a picture of it.
(6) Take your work home and show your family what you found out in school today.

ACTIVITY 2: *(for older/fluent readers)*

(1) Find these two/three books on clothing worn by people in different countries (list of books).
(2) Draw pictures of people in four different countries and read about the clothes they are wearing.
(3) Close the books.
(4) Label your drawings and write short descriptions of the clothes.
(5) Say WHY the clothes are suitable for the people wearing them.
(6) Share your work with your partner.

Your are again invited to extend/develop these activities but you could also examine them in the light of the sequences of skills itemised by Sarah Tann and David Wray. Which skills are being developed? Which are not? How would you change the activities to make them more worthwhile?

The emphasis placed on contextualised skill learning in project work is fully discussed by Wray (1985, pp. 10–11). He points out that there are disadvantages to an 'integrated' approach especially in that there is a danger of skill-learning being left to chance and he advocates whole-school planning to ensure that this does not happen. The advantages of integration, according to Wray, are that:

- skills are taught in relation to actual problems
- they are important and relevant to children
- they are more likely to be put to immediate use

This is, in effect, the way in which the Level 3 SAT operated in 1991. The instructions read as follows:

> In the course of topic or humanities work, ask the children to decide what they need to find out more about.

Ask the children to find or suggest a book that might supply the information.

(SEAC 1991)

The criteria for attaining Level 3 were that the child should think of three things to find out and suggest at least one book where such information could be found.

This integration or relevance is an essential feature of the 'Reading for Learning' project referred to earlier and it is to this that we now turn our attention.

Directed Activities Related to Texts (DARTS)

We have already mentioned that the two Schools Council projects associated with the acronym DARTS were conducted in secondary schools. The first publication, *The Effective Use of Reading* (Lunzer and Gardner, 1979), was a report of research which ran in parallel with the *Extending Beginning Reading* (Southgate *et al.* 1981) study of 7–9 year olds. Basically the aim was to discover how well children in the early secondary years could learn from their reading. Typically a secondary teacher might set a piece of homework which required pupils to read a chapter in a history text-book and answer questions on it the next day. Even when they could read the text they were not very good at answering the questions because they had failed to learn how to extract the important information, facts and key ideas. Many issues impinged on the research – most textbooks, for example, were found to be up to two years more difficult (in readability terms) than the age group for which they were designed.

QUESTION

How true would you say that is of information books for primary children?

A startling finding was that pupils who systematically worked from reading laboratories were more competent readers-for-learning than other children even though such laboratories largely depended on decontextualised traditional passage-plus-question exercises which were being discredited at the time. This, in particular, led to the establishment of a follow-up project designed to investigate and disseminate more dynamic approaches to learning from text and the second report, *Learning from the Written Word* (Lunzer and Gardner, 1984), was the outcome. But even by the time that report was published primary and secondary teachers all over the country were designing and adapting the approaches it described, largely because the dissemination process was well under way by 1981.

Primary teachers became concerned and involved partly because of the earlier findings. Lunzer and Gardner had identified, for example, three main styles of text:

- narrative (stories, etc.)
- expository (information books, etc.)
- instructional (recipes, science books, etc.)

They also outlined three types of reader response:

- receptive (continuous read, e.g. novel)
- reflective (or 'broken read', e.g. consulting a reference book)
- rejective (e.g. text too difficult)

What they found was that children on entry to secondary school, were very proficient at reading *narrative* text in a *receptive* way. That is, they had gained wide experience, in primary school, of reading stories and novels where they started at page one and read on to the end. But many children found difficulty in reading *expository and instructional* texts in a *reflective* way. They tended to read them as they would a story and so they were severely limited in their ability to 'search' the text for key ideas. The second project therefore concentrated on highly teacher-directed methods of helping children to read reflectively and these methods were underpinned by three important principles:

(1) All DARTs should be relevant to work being undertaken in the subject/class.
(2) DARTs should not be worked on by children individually but always in pairs or groups – discussion is an essential part of the process.
(3) There are seldom 'right' or 'wrong' answers to DARTs. Differences of opinion should be discussed and settled by consensus.

The implication of the main findings of the research, so far as primary schools are concerned, was that children could be better prepared for coping with the reading-for-learning demands of secondary education if they gained more experience of reflective reading, via adapted DARTs, at an early age. The bonus for primary schools was that teachers had been struggling against verbatim copying in project work for years and here was a clear framework for counteracting that problem. Now, of course, we are required to develop information retrieval skills by the National Curriculum in the manner outlined earlier in this chapter.

We cannot claim that adapted/simplified DARTs will meet *all* teaching needs in this respect but they do have enormous advantages over published materials in that they are teacher-produced and therefore relevant to the abilities, reading competence and project interests of the children. Consider, for instance, Examples 1, 2 and 3.

Example 1

In Spring we planted
our seeds.
We watered the seeds.

Then the sun shone and
it rained for three days.

Ten days later the plants
started to grow.
They grew and grew.
Then one day we looked out
and saw two flowers.

Our seeds had grown into large flowers.
We watched the flowers
turn brown and dry.
Then we cut them and
collected the seeds

Two sets of cards:

SET A

SET B

Pairs of children read the passage and position the appropriate cards in the frames alongside the relevant parts of the text.

QUESTIONS

Which skills are being developed by these three examples?
How/when might you introduce activities like these into your teaching?
What kind of support would your children need?

Discussion

Example 1 is an *unmodified* (or 'text analysis') DART. A complete passage is presented and children have to locate key ideas, in this case by placing picture or word labels alongside the relevant text.

Example 2

Now they are beginning to look more like frogs. Their tails get shorter.

The tiny tadpoles eat plants in the water. They grow quickly.

After about four weeks the tadpoles start to grow back legs

Tiny tadpoles grow inside the jelly. They wriggle their way out.

When their tails have almost gone they climb out of the water and hop away

Another four weeks go by and their front legs appear.

Pairs of children arrange the cards in a sensible sequence.

A more difficult version would consist of the text alone and instructions to underline, highlight or label certain facts or ideas. This *location* of ideas could then lead to *organisation* on a chart or table and subsequent *reconstruction* where the children wrote about the seeds using only their extracted data – not the original passage. See Lunzer and Gardner (1984) for examples.

Example 1 is a very simple instance of this type of activity. On completion children might re-tell, verbally, what happened using the four cards as cues.

Example 2 is a *modified* (or 'text reconstruction') DART. The life cycle of tadpoles was written by a Year 2 class teacher, cut into six sections and mounted on cards of equal size. On completion the children could relate the sequence in their own words, either verbally or as a picture-caption strip story.

Example 3

THE JOURNEY OF A RIVER

Most rivers have a long journey. They start in hills or mountains and flow downhill until they reach the sea. Some rivers start as marshy ground and others start as springs which gush out of the rocks from underground. All rivers need __rain__ . The rainwater either stays on the surface of the __ground__ to make a marsh or it trickles through the ground to make an __underground__ stream.

The _____ of a river is where it starts as a spring.

A small stream that joins a main stream is called a _____ .

If the river reaches a hollow piece of _____ it fills up the hollow to form a _____ . Some rivers flow swiftly through _____ rocks and wear the _____ away to make a _____ . If the rocks are hard and steep the river makes a _____ .

Eventually the river leaves the hills or _____ and reaches flatter _____ near the coast. That is when the river _____ from side to _____ like the River Thames near _____ .

When there is a great deal of heavy _____ the river gets swollen and bursts its banks on the _____ .

All rivers _____ the sea at their estuary but very large rivers carry sand and soil which build up in the _____ to make small flat islands called a _____ . The River Nile has created a famous _____ . Most of Holland is really the delta of the River _____ which flows through Germany to the _____ Sea.

Pairs of children fill the gaps. The first three gaps were filled during group discussion with the teacher.

Example 3 is another type of modified DART (a 'deletion' DART). The class project on WATER had included models of river valleys and the DART was partly a recap of work already covered, partly an introduction to new knowledge. The Year 5 & 6 children concerned referred to atlases in the latter part of the activity. Note that all the deletion lines are of the same length so as to avoid clues about the lengths of words.

To produce easier versions of the same activity you could:

- vary lengths of lines according to lengths of words
- provide dashes to correspond with letters, e.g. N o r t h
- provide the first letters for some words, e.g. N _ _ _ _
- provide a list of all missing words
- reduce the number of deletions.

The issue of matching the difficulty of a DART to the varying abilities of children in a class is a very important one. A key principle embodied in the National Curriculum, and in special needs education, is that *all children are entitled to access to the whole curriculum*. DARTs provide an excellent opportunity to satisfy this principle because their complexity can be scaled up or down at will. We have indicated how Examples 1 and 3 easily lend themselves to this treatment. Another way is to produce different types of DARTs for different ability groups while still retaining the substance of the information to be learnt. Sequence DARTs (Example 2) are usually easier than Deletion DARTs (Example 3) and both are usually easier than unmodified DARTs – bear in mind that Example 1 is a *very* simple example of such an activity.

All the examples provided here were originally tackled by pairs of children. It is usual to have one pair join another as and when they have completed the activity. These groups then compare their results and agree on a group version. The groups of four children then join others in a 'plenary' discussion to agree the final outcome. Thus the activities involve tightly-structured, highly focussed group discussion and collaboration which in turn provide opportunities to observe and monitor talking/listening as well as social skills. It has also been found that DARTs are highly motivating because they have in-built game and challenge appeal.

In addition to the activities already mentioned, Trevor Cairney (1990, pp. 69–87) provides full details of the following:

- SEMANTIC OUTLINES – identifying and charting main ideas and supporting details.
- TALK-TO-THE-AUTHOR SESSIONS – Photocopies of text on which children note comments and questions.
- ESTIMATE, READ, RESPOND, QUESTION – predict what text will be about, then read it and pose further questions.
- RETELLING – predict what text might be about, read it and retell it to others.
- PROBLEM PROWLING – formulate a question and consult variety of books to arrive at answers.
- PROCEDURAL PROJECT PUZZLERS – inventing instructions for a game/task which is then carried out by others.

- EDITORIAL ARGUMENTS – using newspaper editorials, decide what is/is not agreed with.
- SCHEME PREDICTION – groups predict and then confirm a given text including headings, sub-headings, illustrations, charts etc. Certain computer programs offer similar experiences. 'Developing Tray', for example, is a deletion-type program organised on a game basis and with various levels of complexity (See Chapter Seven).

A very accessible collection of practical suggestions can also be found in David Pryke's *Study Reading* (1991). Ten activities are fully illustrated, described and discussed in a helpful A4 format booklet.

Conclusion

In this chapter attention has been specifically given to the two areas of reading development which HMI have singled out for criticism in recent years. However there are a number of other issues which need to be borne in mind when planning the reading curriculum at Key Stage 2 and some are implicit in the pen-portrait in Chapter One. A major consideration is the organisation of books in the classroom and this featured prominently in the 'Extending Beginning Reading' report (Southgate *et al.* 1981). On the question of readability colour-coding the report concludes:

> Might it not be better (than relying on schemes) to grade the majority of all the books in the school, as simply and speedily as possible, and then allow children to select their own books, at particular levels, according to their own interests? Would not children then be likely to read their books more fluently and more speedily, as well as with pleasure? And would not such a procedure be much more likely to guide them towards permanent habits of reading?
>
> (p. 122)

This feeling was echoed in the HMI Report (1990) when the evidence of infant classes achieving high standards was analysed:

> In almost all the schools progression in reading was structured through the use of books which had been graded into levels of difficulty, usually with a range of readers from different published reading schemes available at each stage. Often these levels were supplemented with non-scheme books to widen the choice. Children read at the level judged appropriate by the teacher and, as their reading improved, they worked through the various levels. (Para 45, p. 9)

The publication which has provided guidance on 'grading into levels of difficulty' for the last twenty years is *Individualised Reading* (Moon, 1992). This continues to list selected reading schemes, paperback children's books, non-fiction and poetry into thirteen stages of difficulty from pure picture books (Stage 0) to books which can be read by top juniors achieving Level 4 in terms of reading fluency (Stage 12) plus additional series for more fluent upper juniors and a list of boxed book packages. The indicative booklists provided in Chapter Six refer to these *Individualised Reading* stages as well as to the *Kaleidoscope Reading Sets* progression which is directly correlated to 'Individualised Reading'. Kaleidoscope Reading Sets, compiled and updated twice annually by Cliff Moon, are distributed by Books for Students, Bird Road, Heathcote, Warwick, CV34 6TB (See Chapter Seven).

QUESTIONS

What else needs to be considered in relation to reading development at Key Stage 2?
Which issues raised in Chapter 4 need further development in the junior years?

CHAPTER 6

Which Books?

The really striking thing about sharing a book with an emergent reader is the extent to which the child's expectation of the text matches what is actually printed. Emergent readers depend heavily if not wholly on illustration and literary cues for they have not yet begun to decipher the words on the page – more advanced emergent readers recognise left to right directionality and sometimes understand one-to-one correspondence. That is, if there are five words accompanying a picture, they will say five words but not necessarily the words that are printed. Yet when you amass a collection of simple illustration-caption books from the early stages of reading schemes and 'real' picture books you find that some texts seldom elicit 'same word' responses from emergent readers whilst others are much more likely to match readers' expectations. It appears that this predictability operates on three levels:

- literary: a robust, sensible narrative
- semantic: the text means something
- syntactic: the printed language is in recognisable written form.

Curiously, the simplest texts we have available seem to demonstrate that authors like Pat Hutchins and Eric Hill are far more likely to produce predictable language than any number of reading scheme starter packs, presumably because the latter are constructed according to a different set of criteria, more particularly that of vocabulary control.

It could be argued that this issue is relatively unimportant because the child is only pretending to read and that concepts about illustration cues, directionality etc. are being developed willy nilly. But what worries us is that concepts like 'print is arbitrary' are also being learnt. An over-riding concern is that opportunities to *teach* are being wasted. When a child 'reads' *Where's Spot?* (Hill 1980) and says:

'In the Clock' for 'Is he inside the Clock?'

the teacher has a chance to intervene with:

'That's right, there's the clock (picture) and *this word says clock*'.

Typically a vocabulary-controlled text would say:

'Is he here?'

and that provides no opportunity to teach anything because there is no match between the text and the child's expectations.

These opening remarks are designed to focus attention on which books are most likely to help children learn to read. By starting with the most rudimentary stages of reading development we can see that this question is not one which applies only to semi-fluent or fluent readers. It is crucial from the start because their first encounters with books and book language form children's attitudes towards reading and their strategies for tackling print. These points are more fully explored in Moon (1986).

When Barrie Wade analysed early reading scheme texts he drew attention to:

> the potential conflict created in the minds of children caused by any reading which promotes arbitrariness instead of pattern, disconnection rather than coherence and emptiness rather than fulfilment.　　　　Wade, 1990, p. 24)

These three criteria: pattern, coherence and fulfilment can serve us well in selecting books for children learning to read. So long as we have books with such qualities in the classroom we can be confident that opportunities for teaching and learning are being maximised.

The acrimonious debate of 1990–91 surrounding the 'real books' issue was largely misconstrued and misunderstood. For one thing the question *Which Books?* was confused with *methods* of teaching reading. The central point seemed to be that alleged falling standards since the mid-eighties could be attributed to a major switch from reading schemes to 'real books' during the same period. Two surveys by NFER and HMI were inconclusive about the falling standards and no evidence was found to support the switch to 'real books'. It emerged that the overwhelming majority of British primary schools used an assortment of resources and teaching approaches much as they had a decade earlier. The Parliamentary Education, Science and Arts Committee, in its May 1991 report, stated:

> Mr. Martin Turner attributed the apparent decline in standards to which he drew attention last year to the growth of the 'real books' methods of teaching reading and the abandonment of the systematic teaching of phonics. We have not found evidence to support this view. (para 29, p.xi)

> **QUESTIONS**
>
> Which books best help *your* children learn to read?
> Which books give you most opportunities to teach your children to read?
> How can you justify the use of 'real books' alongside (or instead of) reading schemes?

The National Curriculum

In fact if schools *are* concentrating expenditure on 'real books' at the present time it is much more likely that they are attempting to meet the requirements of the National Curriculum. The first Cox Report, *English for ages 5 to 11* (DES/WO. 1988b) emphasised the quality of literature to which children should be exposed and the indicative list of suitable authors included eighteen who produce some of the most useful texts for beginner readers:

Petronella Breinburg	Eric Hill	Helen Nicholl
Raymond Briggs	Pat Hutchins	Jan Ormerod
Ruth Brown	Robert Kraus	Helen Oxenbury
John Burningham	Arnold Lobel	Jan Pienkowski
Susanna Gretz	David McKee	Dr. Seuss
Colin & Jacqui Hawkins	Ron Maris	Colin West

This list was prepared for parents of children at an infant school in order to provide guidance when borrowing books from the public library or purchasing books for their children. The remainder of the list is included below:

Picture Book Authors for further developing reading

Janet & Allan Ahlberg	Eric Carle	Florence Parry Heide
Edward Ardizzone	Babette Cole	Helen Piers
Rev. W. Awdrey	Michael Foreman	Beatrix Potter
Stan & Jan Berenstain	Roger Hargreaves	Eve Rice
Leila Berg	Russell Hoban	Tony Ross
Val Biro	Shirley Hughes	Maurice Sendak
Quentin Blake	Judith Kerr	Thomas & Wanda Zacharias
Anthony Browne	Graham Oakley	

Story Book Authors

Janet & Allan Ahlberg	Roald Dahl	Barbara Sleigh
Ruth Ainsworth	Dorothy Edwards	Dick King Smith

Hans Christian Andersen	Norman Hunter	Barbara Softly
Phyllis Arkle	Joseph Jacobs	Catherine Storr
Leila Berg	Geraldine Kaye	Margaret Stuart Barry
Donald Bissett	Ruth Manning Saunders	Jill Tomlinson
Michael Bond	A. A. Milne	Alison Uttley
Jeff Brown	Ursula Moray Williams	
Eileen Colwell	Jill Murphy	
Sara & Stephen Corrin	Pamela Oldfield	
Helen Cresswell	Alf Prøysen	

Poetry was poorly represented in the Cox list but the value of nursery rhymes was stressed and these poets were included:

Janet and Allan Ahlberg	Ogden Nash
Edward Lear	James Reeves
Spike Milligan	Michael Rosen
A. A. Milne	

The list aroused some animosity and was omitted from the second Cox Report, *English for ages 5 to 16* (DES/WO, 1989a). Despite the furore raging at the time the first published SAT for reading at the end of Key Stage 1 (SEAC 1991) was based on suggested children's book titles for emergent readers at Level 1 and required titles for Levels 2 and 3. All these books conform to the label 'real books' although many would prefer to call them 'children's books'. Reading schemes, whatever their merits or short-comings, can only be a means to an end and the end has to be the child's ability to read 'real books'. What the SAT set out to assess was the child's competence in relation to that end.

Thankfully, the Cox Reports avoided the use of labels like 'real books' or 'reading schemes'. They emphasised instead the need to introduce children to a *range* of literature because:

> An active involvement with literature enables pupils to share the experience of others. They will encounter and come to understand a wide range of feelings and relationships by entering vicariously the world of others, and in consequence they are likely to understand more of themselves.
>
> (DES/WO, 1989a, para. 7.3)

The idea of range or breadth of reading surfaces in statements of attainment like:

Level 2: read a range of material with some independence, fluency, accuracy and understanding.
Level 4: read aloud expressively, fluently and with increased confidence from a range of familiar literature.
Level 6: read a range of fiction and poems, explaining in detail their preference by talking and writing.

The programme of study for Key Stage 1 describes what this range might comprise:

> Reading should include picture books, nursery rhymes, poems, folk tales, myths, legends and other literature which takes account of pupils' linguistic competences and backgrounds . . .   (DES/WO 1990, p. 29)

And at Key Stage 2:

> The reading materials provided should include a range of fiction, non-fiction and poetry, as well as periodicals suitable for children of this age. These should include works written in English from other cultures . . .
>   (DES/WO 1990, p. 30)

Range of reading resources: origins

The concept of range implies exposure to different authors and different genres or types of writing. It is not a new idea and, despite the burgeoning of new and existing reading schemes throughout the 1980's, the roots of a broader base to reading resources in primary schools go back much further.

At the turn of the century a psychologist criticised reading schemes on the grounds that 'no trouble has been taken to write what the child would naturally say about the subject in hand' (Huey, 1908), a point which is echoed at the beginning of this chapter. The 1940's and 1950's witnessed two developments, both originating in North America: the design of reading schemes according to vocabulary frequency *and* the child-centred 'individualised reading' movement (See Luke 1988 for a full account). The former prevailed in most schools but in 1970 a London headteacher, Brenda Thompson, published her influential critique of contemporary schemes remarking that:

> There is an astonishing contrast between the almost wilful insipidity of commercial reading text-books and the wealth of appealing illustration in children's picture books in libraries and book shops. . . . There is a grey anonymity about even the best of the reading schemes and it is clear that too much science and too little art goes into the production of 'learning-to-read books.'
>
> (Thompson, 1970 pp. 62–63)

It is recognised that the situation has improved enormously in the intervening period but whilst general appearance and illustration quality may be better, use of language (especially in the early stages) and provision of a range of authorship and genres is, in most cases, severely limited. The Key Stage 2 levels of Longman's 'Reading World' would be one exception mainly because the books consist entirely of anthologies. Yet that brings in question their necessity – why not have the original texts instead? One or two recently published schemes do provide range and visual appeal, for example 'Storychest' (Nelson) and 'Literacy Links' (Kingscourt). Interestingly both schemes originated in New Zealand.

In 1976 Margaret Meek (writing under the surname Spencer) pointed to the double mismatch between the texts beginner-readers are expected to tackle and those that are read aloud to them, as well as the narratives that children have invented during make-believe play during the pre-school years. Both areas of previous experience were being ignored, even negated, by the schools' provision of learning-to-read resources. From her twenty years' scrutiny of children's book publishing (as review editor for the 'School Librarian') she was able to say:

> The crucial difference between the present situation and any that has gone before is illustrated by the extraordinary pressure exerted upon children to become literate, and the incredible wealth of books for young children which exemplify, not the generality of pre-school experience, but the individuality and endless variety and vitality of storytelling. Yet the service of the latter is so little called on to advance the cause of the former. Our most pressing unsolved problem is to define and exemplify the place of children's literature in literacy.
>
> (Spencer, 1976, p. 21)

Margaret Meek's problem did, however, begin to be solved in subsequent years. By 1979 Jill Bennett, a practising infant teacher, had described how she taught reading using children's 'real' books 'right from the start'. Her annotated list of over a hundred 'most useful' books has been regularly updated ever since. Another infant practitioner, Liz Waterland, published the first edition of 'Read with Me' in 1985. This was sub-titled 'An apprenticeship approach to reading' and outlined the classroom organisation, teaching strategies and record-keeping that accompany her use of children's books as learning-to-read resources. Her criteria for book selection are simply that the text should read aloud well and that it . . .

> must have natural language rhythms, the flow of a true story and furthermore must interest the child and the adult.　　　　(Waterland, 1985, pp. 35–36)

Liz Waterland's approach appears to have been over-simplified in some schools as we mention elsewhere but here 'definition and exemplification of the place of children's literature in literacy' is unequalled.

The publication in 1981 of the School's Council Project 'Extending Beginning Reading' lent further weight to the idea of incorporating a range of children's books into the school's reading programme. This project was carried out during the late 1970's and is still the most detailed study of 7–9 year old's reading available. The project team remarked upon the widespread use of schemes and voiced concern at the end of the chapter entitled 'The Books Teachers Use for Teaching Reading':

Are the basic reading schemes being used the ideal reading materials either to grip the children's interests or to increase their reading ability and fluency? Are these schemes such as to convince children that reading is a desirable pursuit?

(Southgate *et al.*, 1981, p. 122)

HMI reports published in 1989 and 1990 drew attention to the breadth of resources for reading. One conclusion states that:

Even in the early years the more fluent and capable readers were sometimes under-challenged, and needed more variety in their reading.

(HMI 1989, p. 16)

And in the more recent report, which was prepared in response to concern about standards, HMI had this to say:

The teachers of classes achieving high standards generally ensured that the children had a wide variety of good reading material in addition to any published scheme or schemes adopted by the school. Moreover the breadth of reading material in these classes was not left to chance. The teachers planned children's reading activities so that they encountered, for example, a good variety of fiction and poetry, read for information from book and non-book sources, read their own and other children's writing, read instructions, signs, maps, lists, indexes, directories, newspapers, magazines, advertisements...

(HMI, 1990 para. 25, p. 6)

Research spanning 25 years has shown that the provision of good books in schools has a positive effect on reading attainment. Joyce Morris' (1966) survey included an analysis of the quantity and quality of reading materials in Kent schools and found that poor standards of reading were associated with poor provision of books. John Downing (1973) found wide variation in the provision of books in schools in 14 different countries. In Denmark and Japan, where the teaching of reading was particularly effective, children had excellent book environments. Warnings of over-reliance on reading schemes have been voiced by Reed (1990) who found that teachers could fall into the trap of entrusting their organisation and teaching to the momentum of the scheme; and by HMI who comment:

... in some schools the programme was too tightly tied to a single published reading scheme. Consequently, many children who were confident within the reading scheme were less secure when challenged to use their reading skills more widely.

(HMI, 1990, para. 26 p. 6)

Fifteen years prior to this the Bullock Report had warned that:

... we regard the reading scheme as an ancillary part of a school's reading programme, and nothing more. We are certainly not advocating that the school should necessarily use one, and we welcome the enterprise of those schools which have successfully planned the teaching of reading without the use of a graded series.   (DES, 1975, para. 7.25)

In order to provide some guidance in the selection of a range of books for primary age children we offer the following selections and indicative lists, arranged in order of children's reading development.

QUESTIONS

What kind of books do you feel you need in your classroom to satisfy the range required by the National Curriculum?
What do you have already?
What else do you need?

Picture Books

Pure Picture Books

There has been a remarkable increase in the availability of picture books, particularly pure picture books, since Margaret Meek posed her 'most pressing unsolved problem'. Publishers used to talk of adults refusing to buy books with few, if any, words because they appeared to represent poor value for money! Maybe Raymond Briggs changed all that – 'The Snowman' certainly broke the ice. Books with no text at all have a special place in the early stages of learning what reading is all about. To begin with the stories they tell are far more complex than anything the child will be able to read for some time to come. Then there are the literary concepts and conventions the child can learn – front to back, left to right directionality. Most importantly the child learns to construct meaning from visual symbolism – a kind of recognition that books offer an extension and enrichment of make-believe. Obviously they will be learning this from hearing stories read aloud but the pure picture book (or a picture book with words which is used like a pure picture book) provides opportunities for children to 'do it for themselves'. The booklist and others which follow consist of recommended selections from recently published paperback editions. Three types of reference are provided:

- National Curriculum fluency levels (approximate guide).
- Individualised Reading stages (Moon, 1992).
- Kaleidoscope Reading Sets (Books for Students).

(Both Individualised Reading and Kaleidoscope Reading Sets are described in detail in Chapter Seven).

BOOKLIST: *Pure Picture Books*

National Curriculum: Working towards Level 1

Individualised Reading: Stage 0

Kaleidoscope Reading Sets: Yellow

Collington, P.	The Angel and the Soldier Boy	Magnet
Dupasquier, P.	Our House on the Hill	Picture Puffin
Prater, J.	The Gift	Picture Puffin
Oakley, G.	Magical Changes	Picturemac
Schubert, D.	Where is Monkey?	Beaver
Smith, R.	Who Goes There?	Dinosaur
Vincent, G.	Breakfast Time, Ernest and Celestine *and* Ernest and Celestine's Patchwork Quilt	Walker Books

---

Caption Books

Books with illustrations and matching captions abound in the early stages of schemes but, as we have seen, the language they use is not always as predictable as it seems. Added to this is the frequent absence of a clear storyline, thereby denying novice readers the opportunity to use literary cues.

The classic example of the genre must be *Rosie's Walk* (Hutchins, 1970), the story of a hen's stroll round the farm pursued by a fox who suffers one misfortune after another. As Jeff Hynds wickedly remarked in a *Books for Keeps* article:

> More happens, on one brief walk, to Rosie and to those who read about her, than happens to Roger Red Hat in a lifetime. (Hynds, 1988)

Of course there *is* much more to Rosie than her brief walk suggests. Does she know she is being followed? If so does she deliberately lead the fox into traps? Is she witless or calculating? And what of her predecessors? It has been suggested that Rosie is a contemporary Red Riding Hood and that the fox is the symbolic predatory male. Unlike Jemima Puddleduck before her, Rosie reaches safety without recourse to a male protector (is that the redundant goat?) A child of her time! Such adult conjecture reveals the 'interpretation at a number of different levels' criterion mentioned in the Cox Report (DES/WO, 1989 a, para. 7.12) and suggests that it appeals to children because it is 'a text which they know means more than it says' (Meek, 1988, p. 24). How can we know the extent of its connection in the

---

BOOKLIST: *Caption Books*

National Curriculum: Level 1

Individualised Reading: Stages 1–6

Kaleidoscope Reading Sets: Yellow

Archbold, T.	The Race	Picture Puffin
Browne, A.	Little Bear Book	Minimac
Browne, A.	I Like Books	Walker Books
Butler, D.	My Brown Bear Barney	Picture Knight
Butterworth, N.	Just Like Jasper!	Picture Knight
Casey, P.	Cluck Cluck	Walker Books
Dale, P.	Bet You Can't	Walker Books
Dowling, P.	Hot Dog	Picture Lion
Galvani, M.	Me and My Cat/Me and My Dog	Picture Puffin
Goode, D.	I Hear a Noise	Little Mammoth
Greeley, V.	Where's My Share?	Picture Lion
Grindley, S.	Four Black Puppies	Walker Books
Hawkins, C. & J.	Busy ABC	Picture Puffin
Hill, E.	Spot Goes to the Farm	Picture Puffin
Maris, R.	Hold Tight, Bear!	Walker Books
Morris, A.	Sleepy Sleepy	Minimac
Ormerod, J.	Just Like Me	Walker Books
Ormerod, J.	My Little Book of Colours/My Little Book of Numbers	Walker Books
Riddell, C.	When the Walrus Comes	Walker Books
Rockwell, A.	Hugo at the Window	Picture Knight
Rockwell, H.	My Kitchen	Walker Books
Smee, N.	Beach Boy	Picture Lions
Thompson, C.	In My Bathroom/In My Bedroom	Walker Books
Van Loan, N.	The Big Fat Worm	Walker Books

---

child's mind with a well known fairy story? This kind of allusion often operates subconsciously and the only indication of its effect is the satisfaction it produces.

Many children will 'know' the text of 'Rosie's Walk' long before they can identify discrete words in other contexts. It will have been read aloud to them and they will have memorised it. That creates the opportunity for, one day, understanding that the 'words in their heads' are the 'words on the page' and the first steps towards independent reading will then have been taken. This can only occur when book language is, in itself, memorable or 'easily memorised'. Such language only arises from a narrative which is told in familiar language accompanying a robust and appealing (to a child) plot.

Or take the linguistic joke about twins Ella and Emily, *Which Witch is Which?* (Hutchins, 1990). The fancy-dressed children play games and eat party food but there is no telling which witch is which, even at the end of the story. There are natural language rhythms with rhyme in places too. There is pattern and coherence and a kind of fulfilment which continues beyond the final question:

> At six o'clock
> they chose a balloon,
> as their parents would be collecting them soon.
>
> Ella chose pink,
> Emily blue.
>
> Which witch is which?

Picture Books with simple text

One Bear in the Picture (Bucknall, 1987) is about Ted being spruced up ready for the school photographer. But he gets splashed on the way to school, eats messily at lunch time, gets muddy at playtime and spills paint in the classroom. By the time the photographer arrives Ted is pretty grubby but when he gets home he bathes without removing his clothes and sits on the radiator to dry. Children find these two pages hilarious, no doubt because they have already identified with Ted and are vicariously enjoying his attempts at concealment. What cannot be concealed is the photographic evidence of the state he had got into and mother's reaction to that is left in the air – an ideal oppoortunity to ask children how they think she will react. This kind of 'What then?' ending provides openings for discussion with individuals, groups and whole classes. Not only are young readers kept in suspense throughout this story but a resolution is withheld at the last moment. Readers must form predictions of their own – an essential facet of fluent reading. A further quality of this book is that its climax is an illustration without text – it provides additional information and therefore complements rather than reiterates the text.

The device of Chinese Whispers is used in *'Can You Keep a Secret?'* by Emma Guenier (1991). Sophie tells her best friend that her sister is keeping a frog in her wardrobe and, by the time seven children have asked each other 'Can you keep a secret?', it emerges that Sophie's sister has a giant hairy fish that lives on a log, swims in the bath and ties its hair in a bow. The linguistic patterning is intricately bound up in similar-sounding words and phrases, the sequence of transmitted secrets comes full circle, back to Sophie, their originator, and the climax is a surprise which might lead to further misunderstandings. In this story we glimpse again what Barrie Wade meant by 'pattern, coherence and fulfilment.'

BOOKLIST: *Picture Books with Simple Text*
National Curriculum: Working within Level 1
Individualised Reading: Stages 7 & 8
Kaleidoscope Reading Sets: Red

Agard, J.	Dig Away Two-Hole Tim	Picture Knight
Allen, P.	Fancy That!	Picture Puffin
Aylesworth, J.	Two Terrible Frights	Picture Puffin
Blake, Q.	Mrs. Armitage on Wheels	Picture Lions
Bourgeois, P.	Big Sarah's Little Boots	Picturemac
Bradman, T.	Wait and See	Little Mammoth
Bradman, T.	In a Minute	Little Mammoth
Chorao, K.	George Told Kate	Picture Corgi
Cole, B.	Cupid	Picture Lions
Cole, B.	Promise and the Monster	Picture Lions
Dodd, L.	A Dragon in a Wagon	Picture Puffin
Fowler, R.	Hugh's Queue	Hippo
Garland, S.	Polly's Puffin	Picture Puffin
Garland, S.	Sam's Cat	Walker Books
Gordon, M.	Getting to Know Cousin Rodney	Walker Books
Grindley, S.	Sardines	Picture Puffin
Harper, A.	What Feels Best?	Picture Puffin
Hawkins, C.	Mr. Wolf's Birthday Surprise	Little Mammoth
Hayes, S.	Bad Egg	Walker Books
Hewett, J.	Rosalie	Picture Puffin
Hill, S.	Suzy's Shoes	Picture Puffin
James, S.	The Day Jake Vacuumed	Picture Piper
Kasza, K.	The Wolf's Chicken Stew	Little Mammoth
Kovalski, M.	The Wheels on the Bus	Picture Puffin
Mayer, M.	There's Something Spooky in my Attic	Picturemac
McMullen, N.	Looking for Henry	Hippo
McPhail, D.	Snow Lion	Little Mammoth
McPhail, D.	Something Special	Picture Puffin
Prater, J.	The Perfect Day	Picture Corgi
Rayner, S.	My First Picture Joke Book	Picture Puffin
Rose, G.	Can Hippo Jump?	Picturemac
Samuels, B.	Duncan and Dolores	Picture Puffin
Smith, M.	Annie and Moon	Picture Puffin
Stafford, M.	Amy's Place	Picture Puffin
Waddell, M.	Once there were Giants	Walker Books
Wells, R.	Shy Charles	Picture Lion
Wells, R.	Max's Chocolate Chicken	Picture Lion
Williams, M.	When I was Little	Walker Books
Willis, V.	The Secret in the Matchbox	Picture Corgi
Ziefert, H.	Let's Swap	Picture Puffin

Picture Books with more complex text

We accept that it is very difficult to tie good books down to a particular reading level but, roughly speaking, some of the books in this category are of similar readability to those in the SAT Level 2 list (SEAC, 1991). *The Sandal* (Badman and Dupasquier, 1989) has been selected as an example partly because it introduces an historical theme. The story is told in two ways: blocks of text and picture strip. The latter is Philippe Dupasquier's preferred style – remember *Dear Daddy...*? We start with a Roman riverside scene in 77 B.C. showing a girl losing her sandal in the river. Then the action switches to 'Today' with a father taking his children for a walk in the city, the park and eventually the museum where they see a Roman sandal in a glass case. On the way home the little girl loses *her* sandal in the river and dad remarks, 'maybe someone will find the sandal one day.' The final sequence, entirely in pictures like the first, depicts a family in a futuristic 2250 A.D., museum looking at the lost sandal.

Katie and the Dinosaur (Mayhew, 1991) is fairly didactic within an overall narrative framework, following Katie's journey through a 'No Admittance' door at the Natural History Museum into a land inhabited by every kind of dinosaur. It is complete with glossary and pronunciation notes and culminates in a 'What next?' ending. Hadrosaurus guides Katie through this intriguing world and she eventually shares her picnic with a mixed party of creatures. Luckily the meat pie she saves for later ends up saving her when she is attacked by Tyrannosaurus Rex. The book ends with Katie dragging her grandma towards the door. Will it still be there? Will the same magic work? A perfect opportunity for children to predict the possibilities posed by the closing words and picture.

The whole-curriculum potential of narratives like this and, for example, the *Lighthouse Keeper* books by Ronda and David Armitage, gives some books a special place in our attempts to prevent fragmentation of the primary curriculum in the wake of the National Curriculum's subject-specific mode of presentation. Some whole-curriculum project work lends itself to the incorporation of stories and poems which support the theme. At other times a book may become the starting point for whole-curriculum work as suggested in *The National Curriculum – making it work for the Primary School* (ASE, 1989) where John Burningham's *Avocado Baby* is mentioned in relation to the topic on 'Food'. The Bright Ideas book, *Using Books in the Classroom* (Short, 1989), sets out examples of ways that fiction, non-fiction and poetry can be harnessed in this way. Also worth noting is *Up and Away* by Michaels and Walsh (1990) who have produced an extremely useful guide to working with picture books in school.

BOOKLIST: *Picture Books with more complex text.*

National Curriculum: Level 2 & Working within Level 2

Individualised Reading: Stages 9 & 10

Kaleidoscope Reading Sets: Blue

Alborough, J.	Beaky	Walker Books
Anderson, S.	Never Keep a Python as a Pet	Hippo
Baker, L.	The Second-Floor Cat	Picture Knight
Beck, I.	The Teddy Robber	Picture Corgi
Brown, K.	Why Can't I Fly?	Picturemac
Brown, M.	Arthur's Christmas	Picture Corgi
Brown, M.	Roll Over D.W.	Picture Corgi
Daniels, U.	The Day the Hippo Landed	Young Knight
De Hamel, J.	Hemi's Pet	Picture Puffin
Dodd, L.	The Smallest Turtle	Hippo
Dupasquier, P.	Robert and the Red Balloon	Walker Books
Geraghty, P.	Over the Steamy Swamp	Red Fox
Gibbons, A.	Our Peculiar Neighbour	Little Mammoth
Gould, D.	Grandpa's Slide Show	Picture Puffin
Gowar, M.	A Hard Day's Work	Picture Puffin
Graham, B.	Crusher is Coming!	Picture Lions
Gray, N.	A Balloon for Grandad	Picture Lions
Himmelman, J.	Montigue on the High Seas	Picture Puffin
Honey, E.	Princess Beatrice and the Rotten Robber	Picture Puffin
Ichikawa, S.	Tanya	Little Mammoth
Keller, H.	The Best Present	Walker Books
Kellogg, S.	Pinkerton, Behave!	Picturemac
Kerr, J.	Mog and Bunny	Picture Lion
Koralek, J. & Gooding, B.	The Friendly Fox	Little Mammoth
Laird, E.	The Inside Outing	Picture Lion
Lionni, L.	It's Mine	Picture Knight
Mahy, M.	The Great White Man-Eating Shark	Picture Puffin
Mogensen, J.	Mary's Christmas Present	Picture Corgi
Moore, I.	Fifty Red Night-Caps	Walker Books
Filling, A.	The Big Biscuit	Young Knight
Rayner, M.	Mrs. Pig's Bulk Buy	Picturemac
Reader, D.	A Lovely Bunch of Coconuts	Walker Books
Richardson, J.	A Dog for Ben	Picture Puffin
Rodgers, F.	The Bunk-Bed Bus	Picture Puffin
Sadler, M.	Alistair Underwater	Picturemac
Smith, R.	Maurice's Mum	Picture Puffin
Smith, W.	Think Hippo!	Picture Puffin
Stevenson, J.	Worse than Willy!	Picture Piper
Talbot, J.	The Dragon's Cold	Walker Books
Todd, H. & Biro, V.	The Silly Silly Ghost	Picture Corgi
Wild, M.	Mr. Nick's Knitting	Picture Knight
Young, J.	Penelope and the Pirates	Picturemac

Picture Books with complex text

The School Trip (Butterworth & Inkpen, 1990) gives a realistic glimpse into the thrills and spills of a coach trip to a museum complete with travel-sick Henry and lunch boxes open before arrival. A few dinosaur facts are slipped in but essentially this is a story that reflects children's personal experiences. They can compare and contrast their own memories of school trips with the one Mrs. Jefferson organises. It is important to remember that children learn about themselves and understand others better from the reflections they glimpse in stories. Elaine Moss wrote movingly about this in *The Cool Web* (Meek *et al.*, 1978) when she described her adopted daughter's passion for a trite tale about Peppermint the kitten. She loved the story because 'she was taken home, like Peppermint, to be cared for and treasured.' (p. 144).

BOOKLIST: *Picture Books with complex text*

National Curriculum: Level 3 & Working within Level 3

Individualised Reading: Stages 11 & 12

Kaleidoscope Reading Sets: Orange

Aardema, V.	Princess Gorilla and a New Kind of Water	Picture Piper
Baillie, A.	Drac and the Gremlin	Picturemac
Bourgeois, P.	Hurry, Up, Franklin	Picturemac
Denman, C.	The Little Peacock's Gift	Picture Corgi
De Paola, T.	The Mysterious Giant of Barletta	Picturemac
Doney, M.	Ears and the Secret Song	Picture Knight
Hedderwick, M.	Katie Morag and the Big Boy Cousins	Picture Lions
Holabird, K.	Angelina and Alice	Picture Puffin
Kennaway, M. & A.	Awkward Aardvark	Picture Knight
Lockwood, P.	Cissy Lavender	Walker Books
Mahy, M.	Making Friends	Picture Puffin
Mayne, W.	Barnabas Walks	Walker Books
Nesbit, E.	Melisande	Walker Books
Oakley, G.	The Dairy of a Church Mouse	Picturemac
Pershall, M.	Hello Barney!	Picture Puffin
Rodgers, P.	Tumbledown	Walker Books
Smith, R.	Looking After Mother	Picture Puffin
Smyth G. & James, A.	A Hobby for Mrs. Arbuckle	Picture Corgi
Todd, H. E.	The Sleeping Policeman	Picture Corgi

Fiction for children of top infant/lower junior ages

The idea of allusions to other stories was mooted when we looked earlier at *Rosie's Walk*. Once children are reading fluently the scope for this 'intertextuality' is much broader and of all contemporary children's authors, no one does it quite as well as the Ahlbergs. The opening of *Jeremiah in the Dark Woods* (Ahlberg and Ahlberg, 1977) illustrates the point admirably:

> Once upon a time there were three bears, seven dwarfs, five gorillas, a frog prince, some sleeping beauties, a wolf, a dinosaur, a Mad Hatter, a steamboat, four firemen on a fire-engine, a crocodile with a clock in it, a considerable number of giant beanstalks – and a little boy named Jeremiah Obediah Jackenory Jones.

Furthermore, Jeremiah's grandma lives in a house made of ginger-bread and cakes, she makes jam tarts for auntie who lives beyond the Dark Woods and leaves them on a window-sill to cool. As you will already have guessed, the tarts get stolen! So how many stories did you identify in that short introduction? Children delight in recognising them too and what of the ones they haven't encountered before? Is it possible that they will come to know Peter's crocodile or Alice's Hatter by reading about them in this story?

Margaret Meek (1988) discusses at some length the way a book like this works to develop children's understanding of story. She analyses *The Jolly Postman*, another classic by the Ahlbergs, and makes this point about it, an observation which equally applies to Jeremiah:

> This intertextuality cannot be a feature of the reading scheme, which offers words to be read only in order to reinforce lessons that are taught *about* reading rather than learned *by* reading. The result is a divergence in competence and understanding between young readers who have entered the reading network through the multiple meanings of polysemic texts and those who may have practised only on the reductive features of words to be 'sounded out' or 'recognised'. Those who have had only the latter experience often feel that they are missing something when they read a text which they know means more than it says. (p. 24).

There is one further thing to note before we leave Jeremiah to his sleuthing. His first encounter in the Dark Woods is with the three bears who are out walking while their porridge cools...

> 'My grandma lost my auntie's tarts while they were cooling,' Jeremiah said.
>
> 'Your grandma is a good grandma, I am sure,' said the father bear. 'But those persons who take tarts from old ladies may well think twice before stealing porridge from a bear.'

Why do children smile at tht point? It can only be that they recognise the irony – they *know* what is happening to the bears' porridge because they know another story. Apart from that important recognition we came across a five-year-old who, after listening to two pages of *Jeremiah*, said 'That's the same as the Jolly Postman!' It is worth reflecting on which lessons these children have learnt from the Ahlbergs.

Two booklists follow, the second for younger children who are very experienced and accomplished readers.

BOOKLIST: *Fiction for children of top infant/lower junior ages*
  National Curriculum: Level 3 & Working within Level 3
  Individualised Reading: Stages 11 & 12
  Kaleidoscope Reading Sets: Orange

Allen, J.	Computer for Charlie	Young Puffin
Blacker, T.	Ms Wiz Stories	Young Piper
Blume, J.	Freckle Juice	Young Piper
Bradman, T.	Gerbil Crazy	Young Puffin
Byars, B.	Beans on the Roof	Young Piper
Cameron, A.	Julian's Glorious Summer	Young Lion
Cave, K.	Poor Little Mary	Young Puffin
Cleary, B.	Here Come the Twins	Young Puffin
Christie, S.	Weedy Me	Young Lion
Crebbin, J.	Finders Keepers	Young Puffin
Cresswell, H.	Greedy Alice	Young Corgi
Dicks, T.	Goliath & the Buried Treasure	Knight
Escott, J.	Wayne's Luck	Young Puffin
Escott, J.	Radio Trap	Young Puffin
Fine, A.	Only a Show	Young Puffin
Hoffman, M.	All about Lucy	Mammoth
Johns, E.	The Three Bears Lend a Hand	Young Corgi
Kaye, G.	Summer in Small Street	Mammoth
King-Smith, D.	The Trouble with Edward	Knight
Lambert, T.	No Holiday Fun for Sam	Young Puffin
Leroy, M.	Aristotle Sludge	Hippo Streamers
Morpurgo, M.	Albertine, Snow Goose	Young Lion
Nash, M.	Enough is Enough	Young Puffin
Newman, M.	Green Monster Magic	Young Corgi
Owen, G.	Douglas the Drummer	Young Lion
Pilling, A.	The Friday Parcel	Young Puffin
Rodgers, F.	Ricky's Summertime Christmas Present	Young Puffin
Thomson, P.	Rhyming Russell	Young Lion
Still, K.	The Tractor Princess	Young Lion
Stuart, J. B. & Stuart, A.	Henry and the Sea	Young Puffin
West, C.	Monty, The Dog who Wears Glasses	Young Lion
Wignell, E.	No Pets Allowed	Young Corgi

BOOKLIST: *More demanding fiction for children of top infant/lower junior ages*

National Curriculum: Levels 4 & 5

Individualised Reading: Beyond Stage 12

Kaleidoscope Reading Sets: Purple

Ball, B.	Stone Age Magic	Young Corgi
Carpenter, H.	Mr. Majeika and the Dinner Lady	Young Puffin
Catling, P. S.	The Chocolate Touch	Mammoth
Corbett, W. J.	Dear Grumble	Mammoth
Counsel, J.	A Dragon in Spring Term	Yearling Books
Crebbin, J.	Ride to the Rescue	Young Puffin
Darke, M.	Night Windows	Piper
Federation of Children's Book Groups	Stories Round the World	Knight
Garvin, J.	I want to be an Angel	Mammoth
Garvin, J.	Kamla & Kate	Mammoth
Gowar, M.	Caroline Columbus	Walker Books
Gurd, L.	Jason Brown – Frog	Young Puffin
Hampshire, S.	Lucy Jane on Television	Mammoth
Kenward, J.	Ragdolly Anna's Treasure Hunt	Young Puffin
Mahy, M.	The Birthday Burglar and A Very Wicked Headmistress	Mammoth
Mahy, M.	The Blood-and-Thunder Adventure on Hurricane Peak	Puffin
Nimmo, J.	Tatty Apple	Mammoth
Pratchett, T.	Diggers	Corgi
Pratchett, T.	Wings	Corgi
Scott, H.	The Summertime Santa	Walker Books
Sefton, C.	Bertie Boggin and the Ghost Again!	Puffin
Smith, R.	Olly	Piper
Smucker, B.	Jacob's Little Giant	Young Puffin
Umansky, K.	Big Iggy	Puffin
Umansky, K.	The Fwog Pwince, the Twuth!	Puffin
Ure, J.	The Wizard in the Woods	Walker Books
Uttley, A.	Foxglove/Rainbow Tales	Young Piper
Walsh, J.	Mr. Shy's Shoes	Yearling Books
Webb, K. (Ed.)	Meet my Friends	Puffin
Williams, U. M.	Grandma and the Ghowlies	Puffin
Williams, U. M.	Tiger Nanny	Red Fox
Wilson, D. H.	Yucky Ducky	Piper
Wilson, D. H.	Gander of the Yard	Piper
Wilson, J.	Glubbslyme	Yearling Books

Fiction for junior age children

Once children are able to read fluently they need access to the enormous range of fiction which is available for this age group. The full indicative list of authors presented in *English for ages 5 to 11* (DES/WO, 1988(b)) provides a useful starting point but new authors are continually making their debut and in recent years there has been an influx of excellent novels from Australian writers. Reviews in *Books for Keeps* and *School Librarian* are a good way of keeping up-to-date with recent publications.

Two books serve to illustrate the qualities we should be seeking. Dick King-Smith enjoys deserved popularity with juniors. As an ex-farmer turned primary teacher he can claim to know something about animals and children. *Saddlebottom* (King-Smith, 1985) is viewed as a huge disappointment by Dorothea, his mother, because his white patch is not where it should be. He takes the old rat's advice and decides to run away to save his bacon! Immediately there are shades of Pigling Bland and Wilbur, the kinds of allusion we mentioned earlier. The magic begins to work.

Anne Fine writes a completely different kind of novel, concentrating on growing pains and social/emotional problems. Hers are books 'you can't put down' if you happen to be an upper junior (or adult!) who can empathise with her characters. Yet she avoids bathos by well-paced narrative and gentle fun-poking which pre-pubescent children find both amusing and comforting. *Goggle-Eyes* (Fine, 1989) deals with Kitty's coming-to-terms with her mother's new boyfriend – she tells her story to Helly Johnson in the school's lost property cupboard after Helly has stormed from the classroom during registration. The description of Kitty's chaotic bedroom (pp. 41–45 in the Puffin edition) must be one of the funniest passages in the book and one with which top juniors very readily identify!

It must be emphasised that the following booklists represent only a limited selection from recently published paperback fiction for this age group.

BOOKLIST: *Fiction for junior-age children*

National Curriculum: Level 3 and Working within Level 4

Individualised Reading: Stages 11 & 12

Kaleidoscope Reading Sets: Green

Ahlberg, A.	Ten in a Bed	Puffin
Ashley, C.	You can be Spurs	Walker Books
Brown, J.	Stanley in Space	Mammoth
Catling, P. S.	The Orphan and the Billionaire	Mammoth
Childs, R.	The Big Kick	Young Corgi
Cleary, B.	Henry and Beezus	Puffin
Cole, H.	Kick-off	Walker Books
Curtis, P.	Mr. Browser and the Space Maggots	Puffin
Dicks, T.	Jonathon's Ghost	Red Fox
Fisher, C.	The Conjuror's Game	Red Fox
Fisk, N.	The Talking Car	Mammoth
Geras, A.	The Magic Camera	Young Corgi
Greenwald, S.	The Secret in Miranda's Wardrobe	Puffin
Gregory, P.	Princess Forizella	Puffin
Hamley, D.	Hare's Choice	Lions
Hayashi, N.	Cosmic Cousin	Red Fox
Hill, D.	Penelope's Pendant	Piper
Jones, D. W.	Who Got Rid of Angus Flint?	Mammoth
King-Smith, D.	Martin's Mice	Puffin
King-Smith, D.	Lightning Strikes Trice	Mammoth
King-Smith, D.	Paddy's Pot of Gold	Puffin
King-Smith, D.	Dodos Are Forever	Puffin
Lively, P.	Uninvited Ghosts	Mammoth
Matthews, A.	Mallory Cox & his Magic Socks	Knight
Mayne, W.	Kelpie	Puffin
Mayne, W.	The Farm that Ran Out of Names	Red Fox
Morgan, A.	Staples for Amos	Walker Books
Needle, J.	In the Doghouse	Mammoth
Richemont, E.	The Time Tree	Walker Books
Shemin, M.	The Little Riders	Walker Books
Smith, J.	The Russian Doll	Walker Books
Smith, N.	Will You Come on Wednesday?	Walker Books
Stevenson, J.	O'Diddy	Red Fox
Warburton, N.	Saving Grace	Mammoth
Wiseman, D.	Jumping Jake	Yearling Books
Woods, S.	Now then, Charlie Robinson	Puffin

BOOKLIST: *More demanding fiction for junior-age children.*

National Curriculum: Level 4 to 5

Individualised Reading: Beyond Stage 12

Kaleidoscope Reading Sets: Brown

Banks, L. R.	The Secret of the India	Lions
Bawden, N.	The Outside Child	Puffin
Bernard, P.	Kangaroo Kids	Corgi
Bevan, C.	Mightier than the Sword	Puffin
Brennan, J.J.	Shiva	Armada
Cate, D.	Foxcover/Twisters	Yearling Books
Clement, A.	The Cold Moons	Puffin
Cole, H.	In at the Shallow End	Walker Books
Dunn, C.	Just Nuffin	Red Fox
Fine, A.	A Pack of Liars	Puffin
Fox, P.	The Lost Boy	Piper
Fox, P.	In a Place of Danger	Lions
Gee, M.	The Champion	Puffin
Henshall, D.	Starchild and Witchfire	Firefly (Macmillan)
Herlihy, D.	Ludie's Song	Puffin
Howard, E.	Edith Herself	Lions
Jacques, B.	Mattimeo	Arrow-Red Fox
Kemp, G.	Just Ferret	Puffin
Laird, E.	Red Sky in the Morning	Piper
Lively, P.	The Voyage of QV66	Mammoth
Lowry, L.	Number the Stars	Lions
McCaughren, T.	Run with the Wind/Run to Earth	Puffin
Morpurgo, M.	War Horse	Mammoth
Nimmo, J.	Snow Spider Trilogy	Mammoth
O'Neill, J.	Stringybark Summer	Mammoth
Paulsen, G.	Hatchet	Piper
Pilling, A.	Our Kid	Puffin
Sampson, F.	The Free Man on Sunday	Lions
Smith, R. K.	Bobby Baseball	Piper
Sutcliff, R.	Flame-Coloured Taffeta	Puffin
Swindells, R.	Room 13	Yearling Books
Townsend, J. R.	The Golden Journey	Puffin
Trease, G.	Tomorrow is a Stranger	Piper
Voight, C.	Tree By Leaf	Lions

Criteria for selection of picture books and fiction

The books referred to in the preceding sections demonstrate a range of qualities and these can be summarised as follows:

- memorable language
- suspense
- humour
- illustrations which complement the text
- reflection of a child's world – opportunities for empathising with characters
- intertextuality – opportunities for identification at more than one level of interpretation
- some opportunities for integration with whole-curriculum planning.

The second Cox Report (DES/WO, 1989a) suggests the following criteria in selecting books for primary aged children:

> Para. 7.12 The language used should be accessible to children but should also make demands and extend their language capabilities. In fiction, the story should be capable of interpretation at a number of different levels, so that children can return to the book time and again with renewed enjoyment in finding something new. Most important, the books selected must be those which children enjoy.
>
> Para. 7.13 Print should be bold and easy to read. Illustrations should be clear and attractive and, as well as being well-matched and giving helpful clues to the text, should enhance it by providing additional information, for example about the characters or setting.

Non-statutory Guidance (NCC 1990) suggests further that:

> In selecting books, teachers should note the quality of design and illustration, the interest of the narrative and the accessibility of the information. (B5)
>
> Reading texts which make sense of life and explore feelings help children to become active readers. (D1)
>
> Memorable language and interesting content are the distinguishing features of good quality texts. (D1)

We must add to these excellent criteria others which address the problems of cultural stereotypes, for the white male middle-class character is still a pervasive feature in children's books of all kinds. We should be concerned that every child has the right to find him or herself in a book, otherwise perceptions of self-worth as well as attitudes towards reading may be subtly affected.

Here are some of the things to look for:

- books which depict children from non-white ethnic groups in central roles

- books which depict females in central roles, especially where the characters are animals rather than humans
- books which have inner urban rather than suburban settings
- dual-language and mother tongue books (for *all* children so that they learn to value languages which are different from English)
- books which depict one-parent families
- books which show people engaged in manual and industrial occupations.
- books which show non-stereotypical images of working people (eg. male nurse, female lorry driver)
- books which depict quiet, sensitive boys and active, aggressive girls (or male/female animals)
- books which show grandparents as middle-aged, attractive and employed (the stereotypical grandparent often looks more like a great-grandparent!)

See Sandra Smidt (1985) for a very valuable chapter which contains many suggestions and addresses of specialist bookshops stocking books from a variety of countries.

Other useful references include:

Baker, C. D. & Freebody, P. (1989) *Children's First School Books*, Blackwell.
Klein, G. (1985) *Reading into Racism: Bias in Children's Literature and Learning Materials*, Routledge & Kegan Paul.
Klein, G. (1985) *The School Library for Multicultural Awareness*, Trentham Books.
Stones, R. (1983) *Pour the Cocoa Janet: Sexism in Children's Books*, Longman for Schools Council.

We would recommend the following dual-language books and series:

- *All About Me* series published by Blackie.
- Collections of traditional Asian and European folktales published by Edward Arnold (eg *The Mango Tree and other Tales of Greed)*.
- *Ducts* series published by Hamish Hamilton.
- Harmony Publishing Company – produces books plus accompanying cassettes (eg. *Topiwalo the Hat-Maker*, *Sameep and the Parrots*, *Sonal Splash*).
- Ingham Yates Dual Language Books (eg. *Dear Zoo*, *Not Now Bernard*, *The Ugly Duckling*).
  (From: Ingham Yates Ltd., 40, Woodfield Road, Rudgwick, Horsham, West Sussex, RH12 3EP).
- Luzac Storytellers Series comprises over 70 titles including folk tales, fables, 'tall tales', '*Akbar & Birbal*' stories and '*Young Storytellers*' published by Andre Deutsch.
- Macdonald Starters are published in dual-language versions.

- Magi Publications (in association with Star Books International, 55, Crowland Avenue, Hayes, Middlesex UB3 4JP) have recently published *I Want My Potty* by Tony Ross in Chinese and English, Vietnamese and English and Spanish and English (1991, £6.99 each).
- Mantra Publishing produce *'Arjuna's Family'* and *Sunnita* series.
- Tiger Books produce the *Panchatantra Series* edited by Sushil Sharma – available from 18 Thirlmere Avenue, Perivale, Middlesex, UB6 8EF.

Books published in languages other than English are available from:

- Commonwealth Institute bookshop which stocks a variety of books and materials.
- Nelson: *City Kids* series (8 packs of 6 books in Greek, Italian, Turkish, etc.)
- Soma Books have a large selection imported from various countries: Soma Books, Independent Publishing Co., 38, Kennington Lane, London, SE 11 4LS
- Letterbox Library is a source of non-sexist and multi-cultural books for children. A catalogue is available from: Letterbox Library, 8 Bradbury Street, London, N16 8JN

NOTE: Also see Chapter Seven.

Poetry

> As children read more, write more, discuss what they have read and move through the range of writing in English, they amass a store of images from half-remembered poems, of lines from plays, of phrases, rhythms and ideas. Such a *reception* of language allows the individual greater possibilities of *production* of language. (DES, 1988, p. 11)

Poetry is probably the nearest that written language can get to the natural rhythms of a child's life. It has even been suggested that the pulse of rhyme echoes the pre-natal beat of a mother's heart and that the knee-jogging games of early childhood are able to quieten a distressed baby for this very reason.

Jingles like 'This little piggy went to market' and 'This is the way the farmer rides' provide an early introduction to the way in which language can be manipulated to provide pleasure and comfort. Indeed Michael Benton and Geoff Fox (1985, p. 82) talk about 'language as a plaything' and they assert that 'the priority must be the experience of poetry as fun'. They go on to say that it is:

> ...vital that children become aware that poetry can be written about anything from dustbins to the cosmos, that it has many voices and reflects

many different moods; that it is often jokey and not too different from the rhymes and jingles, jokes and puns that are part of every childhood – yet, in its mystery, it can also command stillness and wonder. (p. 77)

Benton and Fox claim that to experience poetry is to experience 'language at its most condensed and imaginative' and that through poetry we are able to discover how feelings are shaped. Dougill and Knott (1988, p. 57) list four areas of learning that accrue from close contact with poetry:

– increased awareness of how language works
– greater precision in the use of language through compression
– increased awareness of language through illusion and imagery
– development of the imagination.

So what kinds of poetry should children encounter? It is generally agreed that three main genres are particularly appropriate to the primary age range:

● fun poems, comic verse, nonsense poetry
● poems that teach, didactic verse
● lyrical and story poems.

Several commentators add that children should be introduced to poetry from what Roger Beard (1990, p. 182) calls 'eminent legacies' but these can be subsumed under the three genres listed above if we include poets like Lear, Carroll, T. S. Eliot, Longfellow, Coleridge, Rosetti and Walter de la Mare.

Anne Rowe has listed and annotated recommended poetry books in *101 Good Poetry Books*, published by the Reading and Language Information Centre, University of Reading, 1989.

The following lists comprise currently available collections of poetry which include old favourites as well as some which have been published more recently. They are indicative of the range we should aim to provide both for reading aloud to children and for children's independent reading. Paperback publishers are given wherever possible.

BOOKLIST: *Poetry for Infants*

Aardema, Verna	Bringing the Rain to Kapatiti Plain	Picturemac
Agard, John	I Din Do Nuttin	Magnet
Agard, John	Say it Again, Granny	Magnet
Agard, John & Nichols, Grace	No Hickory, No Dickory, No Dock	Viking
Ahlberg, Janet & Allan	Each Peach Pear Plum	Picture Puffin
Bennett, Jill (Ed.)	Singing in the Sun	Young Puffin
Bradman, Tony	All Together Now	Young Puffin
Bradman, Tony	Hissing Steam and Whistles Blowing	Young Puffin
Bradman, Tony	The Best of Friends	Young Puffin
Causley, Charles	Early in the Morning	Puffin
Corrin, S. & S.	Once upon a Rhyme	Young Puffin
Edwards, R.	If Only . . .	Young Puffin
Foster, John (Ed.)	A Very First Poetry Book	O.U.P.
Ireson, Barbara	Young Puffin Book of Verse	Young Puffin
Longfellow, H.	Hiawatha	Picturemac
Magorian, M.	Waiting for my Shorts to Dry	Picture Puffin
Matthias, Beverley & Bennett, Jill (Eds)	Pudmuddle Jump In	Magnet
Milne, A. A.	Now we are Six	Methuen
Milne, A. A.	When we were very young	Methuen
Nicoll, Helen (Ed.)	Poems for 7 year olds and under	Young Puffin
Rosen, Michael	Don't Put Mustard in the Custard	Picture Lion
Rosen, Michael	Mind Your Own Business	Lion
Rosen, Michael & Oxenbury, Helen	We're Going on a Bear Hunt	Walker
Rosen, Michael	You Can't Catch Me	Picture Puffin
Rumble, Adrian (Ed.)	Sit on the Roof and Holler	Young Puffin
Stevenson, R. L.	A Child's Garden of Verses	Puffin
Stones, Rosemary & Mann, Andrew	Mother Goose Comes to Cable Street	Picture Puffin
Styles, Morag	I Like that Stuff	C.U.P.
Styles, Morag	You'll Love this Stuff	C.U.P.

BOOKLIST: *Poetry for Juniors*

Agard, John	Laughter is an Egg	Puffin
Ahlberg, Allan	Please Mrs. Butler	Puffin
Ahlberg, Allan	Heard it in the Playground	Viking Kestrel
Belloc, Hillaire	Selected Cautionary Verses	Puffin
Berry, James	When I Dance	Puffin
Causley, Charles	Figgie Hobbin	Macmillan
Causley, Charles	Jack the Treacle Eater	Picturemac
Causley, Charles	The Young Man of Cury	Macmillan
Cole, W.	Beastly Boys & Ghostly Girls	Methuen
Cole, W.	Oh, How Silly	Methuen
Cole, W.	Oh, That's Ridiculous	Methuen
Cole, W.	What Nonsense?	Methuen
Dahl, Roald	Revolting Rhymes	Picture Puffin
de la Mare, Walter	Peacock Pie	Puffin
Edwards, Richard	A Mouse in My Roof	Puffin
Edwards, Richard	The Word Party	Young Puffin
Eliot, T. S.	Old Possum's Book of Practical Cats	Faber
Foster, John (Ed.)	First, Second, Third, Fourth, Fifth Poetry Books	O.U.P.
Graham, Eleanor (Ed.)	Puffin Book of Verse	Puffin
Harvey, Anne (Ed.)	Faces in a Crowd	Puffin
Hughes, Ted	Meet My Folks	Puffin
Hoban, R.	The Pedalling Man	Heinemann
Hughes, Ted	Moonbells and Other Poems	Bodley Head
Magee, Wes	Madtail Miniwhale	Puffin
McGough, Roger	Pillow Talk	Viking Kestrel
McGough, Roger	Sky in the Pie	Puffin
McGough, Roger & Rosen, Michael	You Tell Me	Puffin
McNaughton, Colin	There's an Awful Lot of Weirdos in Our Neighbourhood	Walker
Milligan, Spike	Startling Verse for all the Family	Puffin
Milligan, Spike	Unspun Socks from a Chicken's Laundry	Puffin
Nichols, Grace	Come on into my Tropical Garden	A. & C. Black
Nicholls, Judith	Magic Mirror	Faber
Nicholls, Judith	Midnight Forest	Faber
Owen, Gareth	Salford Road	Lion
Owen, Gareth	Song of the City	Young Lion
Patten, Brian	Gargling with Jelly	Puffin
Prelutsky, Jack	The Walker Book of Poetry for Children	Walker
Rosen, Michael	The Hypnotiser	Andre Deutsch

BOOKLIST: *Poetry for Juniors.* CONTINUED

Rosen, Michael	Wouldn't You Like to Know	Puffin
Rumble, Adrian (Ed.)	Shadow Dance	Puffin
Scannell, V.	Travelling Light	Bodley Head
Snell, Gordon	Hysterically Historical	Arrow
Untermeyer, Louis (Ed.)	The Golden Treasury of Poetry	Collins
West, Colin	What would you do with a Wobble-dee-woo?	Puffin
Wright, Kit	Cat Among the Pigeons	Puffin
Wright, Kit	Hot Dog	Puffin
Wright, Kit (Ed.)	Poems for Nine Year Olds and Under/Poems for Ten Year Olds and Under	Young Puffin

Folk and fairy tales, myths and legends

> Reading should include picture books, nursery rhymes, poems, folk tales, myths, legends and other literature which takes account of pupils' linguistic competences and backgrounds. (Programme of Study for Key Stage 1, DES/WO 1990, p. 29)

The inclusion of 'folktales, myths and legends' in the National Curriculum's definition of *range* is partly so that children will come to understand allusions when they encounter them in their general reading (remember Jeremiah?) and so learn to understand 'literary heritage'. It is also partly that they should be led to 'a broader awareness of a greater range of human thought and feeling' (DES/WO, 1989a, para. 7.5). Above all, stories which have been honed by centuries of oral re-telling do have the edge on younger narratives. They are spare, refined, dynamic and contain a great deal of 'memorable language' ...

> Oh Grandma, what big eyes you've got ...
> Little pig, little pig, let me come in ...

There are many anthologies, mostly superbly illustrated, which can be read aloud to children at storytime. There is something especially magical about openings like:

> Once upon a time ...
> Long ago there was once ...
> There was in ancient times ...
> In the golden age of the Caliph ...
> It is said that in a certain city in China ...

A particular favourite is Alan Garner's (1984) re-tellings of British Fairy Tales illustrated by prints cut by Derek Collard. The Lincolshire story 'Yallery Brown' opens:

> I've heard tell as how the boggles and boggarts were main bad in the old times, but I can't rightly say as I ever saw any of them myself, not rightly boggles, that is, but I'll tell you about Yallery Brown. (p. 33)

Garner's introduction to the collection contains some excellent pointers to the qualities we should seek when selecting this genre for children:

> Plot evolves through physical action, and other concerns are kept in the listener's head by repetition...the meaning is in the music; it is in the language: not phonetics, grammar or syntax, but pitch and cadence, and the colour of the word. (p. 7)

Edna O'Brien's (1988) Irish stories certainly sing as do James Riordan's (1983) *Tales from the Arabian Nights.*

The booklist suggestions which follow are not drawn from such anthologies at all – those are plentiful in bookshops and libraries. The emphasis in these lists is on stories children can read for themselves and they are culled from paperback editions and inexpensive series published by educational publishers. These, and others like them, can provide the basis for classroom collections. In order to 'take account of pupils' linguistic competencies' *Individualised Reading* stages have been included. One way to extend the imaginative experience of novice readers is to read aloud a 'difficult' version from an anthology and match it with a simpler version which the children can read for themselves afterwards. In this way they can recall the richer fabric of the read-aloud story as they successfully rehearse their own.

For example: *The Twelve Dancing Princesses* (Ehrlich, 1986)

> Once there was a king who had twelve daughters and each was more beautiful than the next. They slept side by side in a great hall that he locked and bolted each night.... (p. 34)

The Twelve Dancing Princesses (Moon, 1988)

> Once upon a time
> there was a king who had
> twelve beautiful daughters.
> They had twelve beds
> in one big room and
> every night the door was locked. (p. 2)

BOOKLIST: *Folk and Fairy Tales, Myths and Legends.*

(1) Individual paperback editions.

Author	Title	Publisher	Individualised Reading Stage
Andersen, H. C.	The Wild Swans	Walker Books	12
Berry, J.	A Thief in the Village	Puffin	12
Charles, F. (Ed.)	Under the Storytellers Spell	Puffin	12
Denman, C.	The Little Peacock's Gift	Picture Corgi	11
De Paola, T.	The Mysterious Giant of Barletta	Picturemac	11
Federation of Children's Book Groups	Stories Round the World	Knight	12
Gray, N.	The One and Only Robin Hood	Walker Books	9
Grimm Bros.	Hansel and Gretel	Picturemac	11
Hallworth, G.	Mouth Open Story Jump Out	Magnet	12
Hastings, S.	Sir Gawain and the Green Knight	Walker Books	Beyond stage 12
Lester, J.	The Adventures of Brer Rabbit	Piper	12
Marshall, J.	Goldilocks and the Three Bears	Picture Lion	10
Mayer, M.	East of the Sun and West of the Moon	Picturemac	11
Steptoe, J.	Mufaro's Beautiful Daughters	Hodder & Stoughton	12
Wilde, O.	The Selfish Giant	Walker Books	12
Windham, S.	Noah's Ark	Picturemac	9

BOOKLIST: *Folk and Fairy Tales, Myths and Legends.*

(2) Series.

Series Title	Publisher	Individualised Reading Stage
Fables from Aesop	Ginn	7 & 8
Folk Tales of the World	Blackie	11
Great Tales from Long Ago	Methuen	11
Once upon a Time	Ginn	7 & 8
Tales from Hans Andersen	Ginn	9
Traditional Tales from Around the World	Ginn	12
World Legends	Usborne	10

Non-fiction

The Reading Attainment Target's requirement, 'development of information-retrieval strategies for the purposes of study' leads to renewed scrutiny of available non-fiction. Statements of Attainment talk about 'appropriate information sources and reference books from the class and school library' (Level 3).

The programme of Study for Key Stage 1 is more specific:

> Non-fiction texts should include those closely related to the word of the child and extend to those which enable children to deepen an understanding of themselves and the world in which they live, e.g. books about weather, wildlife, other countries, food, transport, the stars, (DES/WO, 1990, para. 3, p. 29)

There have been many problems in the past with primary non-fiction and these have been overcome only to a limited extent in recent years despite a deluge of series designed to assist delivery of the National Curriculum. Principally the supply of suitable simple texts for infants has always been sparse and books for juniors are frequently much more difficult to read than appears at first sight. Hill (1978) surveyed a sample of junior school library books and found non-fiction to be much more difficult than fiction. Paice (1985) p. 49 related an amusing story from her infant classroom:

> I have a book about bees which shows a mass of them on the comb. The title is *The Bee*. A child asked me, 'Which one?'

Bobbie Neate (1988) conducted a detailed investigation into junior information books and concluded that although presentation had improved since 1980, 'text and structure of the books is basically left to chance' (p. 45). She is particularly critical of what she calls 'anomalous linguistic register'; that is, the written style of children's information books is not only very varied from book to book but also *within* books. She believes that a 'straightforward informational register is best'. Neate also found that the *theme* sometimes switches quite alarmingly – in one book she cites there are four distinct themes in a 50 word extract! She makes a special plea for more widespread use of 'structural guiders' to enable children to *refer to* information books rather than being forced, by virtue of their presentation, to read them from beginning to end. Structural guiders include an introduction, book or chapter summaries, cover blurb, contents page, index, bibliographies, glossary, headings and sub-headings.

Katherine Perera (1984) raised an important issue regarding the development of children's ability to *write* factual accounts for themselves. Because the linguistic register of such writing is found in neither speech nor narrative text, the only way children can internalize the necessary forms is by hearing non-fiction read aloud or by reading it themselves:

> It is particularly important for pupils to read extended passages of good non-fiction so that they acquire a feeling for the overall organisation of such discourses and not just for sentence-level details of vocabulary and grammar.
>
> (Perera, 1984, pp. 266–7).

According to Paice (1985, p. 47) the purposes of non-fiction reading are:

For beginner readers

– consolidation of known facts
– introduction to the genre of non-fiction.

For fluent readers

– ordering and organizing information
– learning new information of their own choice.

The following questions may be useful when selecting non-fiction for primary children

● Can the children read it?
● Is the subject matter appropriate?
● What will it teach the children?
● How can the children use it?
● What is it better or worse than?
● Will it stimulate children's curiosity?
● Will it lead to first hand research and practical activities?

You should also pay particular attention to:

- directness and suitability of style
- position and explicitness of illustrations and diagrams
- relationships between ideas.

The last point is especially relevant in view of the publishers' penchant for double-page spread designs – some books are only coherent within each double spread and every page turn lurches to a new topic.

The following two booklists comprise fairly recently published non-fiction series. The shortage of easily accessible texts is demonstrated by the inclusion of *Individualised Reading* stages (Stage 9 is approximately equivalent to SAT level 2 readability) and it is also obvious that production of reliable series is largely in the hands of a few publishers like Black, Firefly, Heinemann, Usborne, Watts and Wayland. It has to be stressed that few of the series listed will completely satisfy every criterion mentioned above.

One further point to note is that some of the newer reading schemes include non-fiction in their range and some of these books are aimed at younger children. The following are worth inspection:

Book Bus	Collins
Highgate Collection	Harcourt Brace Jovanovich
Sunshine	Heinemann

BOOKLIST: *Selected Series of Non-fiction for Infants.*

Series Title	Publisher	Individualised Reading Stage
Animal Readers	Firefly	7
Castles	Firefly	8
Dinosaur Readers	Firefly	8
Family Life	Firefly	8
Farm/Home/Street Noises	Firefly	9
First Learning Library	Blackwell	7
Ginn History	Ginn	8
Giraffe Books	Hodder & Stoughton	8
Healthy Living	Wayland	9
I Am A . . . series	Kingfisher	7
If I could be an Animal	Ginn	5
Living Long Ago	Usborne	9
Look at Nature	Watts	9

BOOKLIST: *Selected Series of Non-fiction for Infants. Continued*

Series Title	Publisher	Individualised Reading Stage
Make and Discover	Collins	9
My Book About . . .	Wayland	8
My First Look at . . .	Heinemann	7
Nature Stories	Ginn	7
Outings	Firefly	6
People Who Help Us	Wayland	8
Science Activities	Usborne	9
Science Around Us	Usborne	9
Science Safari	Black	9
Science Story Books	Ginn	6 & 7
See How They Grow	Dorling Kindersley	7
Simple Science	Black	7
Starting Maths	Wayland	9
Starting Point Science	Usborne	9
Starting Science	Wayland	9
Starting Technology	Wayland	9
Take One	Simon & Schuster	7
Your Senses	Wayland	9
Watch Out	Wayland	9
Ways to . . .	Watts	8

BOOKLIST: *Selected Series of Non-fiction for Juniors.*

Series Title	Publisher	Individualised Reading Stage
Alternative Energy	Wayland	12
Animals Around Us	Usborne	11
Celebrations	Wayland	10
Century of Change	Hodder & Stoughton	11
Conservation Guides	Usborne	11
Earthwatch	Black	12
Exploring Technology	Wayland	12
Farming Now	Hodder & Stoughton	12
First Facts	Heinemann	11
First History	Usborne	10
First Pets	Watts	11

BOOKLIST: *Selected Series of Non-fiction for Juniors.* continued

Series Title	Publisher	Individualised Reading Stage
First Sight	Black	10
Flying Start	Wayland	10
Food	Wayland	10
Great Journeys/Lives	Wayland	12
Green World	Heinemann	12
Health Facts	Heinemann	11
History of Britain	Nelson	12
Houses and Homes	Wayland	11
Jane Goodall's Animal World	Collins	11
Life Cycle	Wayland	10
Links	Wayland	11
Living History	Wayland	10
Looking at Transport	Wayland	10
Looking Back at . . .	Heinemann	12
Magic Beans In-Fact Series	H. B. J.	11
Media in Action	Heinemann	12
Media Story	Wayland	11
My Sport	Watts	11
Mysteries & Marvels	Usborne	12
Nature Club	Eagle Books	12
Nature Study	Wayland	10
Operation Earth	Black	12
Our Country	Wayland	12
Our Green World	Wayland	11
People of the World	Wayland	11
Picture World History	Usborne	11
Pioneers in History	Black	12
Rebuilding the Past	O.U.P.	12
Science Now	Heinemann	12
Seasonal Weather	Wayland	12
Signs and Symbols	Wayland	11
Story of Britain	MacMillan	11
Then and Now	Ginn	10
Through the Seasons	Wayland	10
Turn of the Century	Black	12
Way we Live	Evans	11
Young Researcher	Heinemann	12
Your Health	Wayland	11

QUESTIONS

What are the qualities to look for in picture books, fiction, folk/fairy tales, myths and legends, poetry, non-fiction?

What sort of lessons do children learn *about* reading from the books available to them?

What sort of criteria do you have in mind when you select books for your classroom?

Readability

The Bullock report asserted that:

> ...a particularly important teaching skill is that of assessing the level of books by applying measures of readability. The teacher who can do this is in a better position to match children to reading materials that answer their needs...
>
> The effective teacher is one who has under her conscious control all the resources than can fulfil her purpose. By carefully assessing levels of difficulty she can draw from a variety of sources. (DES, 1975, para. 7.32)

The procedure for assessing the readability of books listed in *Individualised Reading* is one of trial and error with children in Primary Schools. Their teachers monitor the fluency of their reading – books which can be read with similar fluency are grouped together and eventually assigned to stages in the published lists. But whilst that pragmatic procedure works well enough for our purposes it tells us nothing about the print factors which *cause* a book to be hard or easy for a child to read. Some knowledge of such causes is useful partly because it aids book selection and partly because it helps to explain what might be interfering with a child's reading fluency during, for example, a read-aloud-to-teacher session.

Readability formulae have been available for many years and teachers often ask why these are not used for *Individualised Reading* assessment. The difficulty here is the level of text we are dealing with. Most formulae come into their own at the point where *Individualised Reading* stages finish. They are ideal for adult text, journals, official forms and instructions. They have limited value with children's books because they take no account of illustrations nor of the reader's previous knowledge and experience. Most of them are solely concerned with two variables – length of word and length of sentence. We can all think of short words and sentences which are very difficult to read and, similarly, there are some very long words and sentences which children cope with extremely well. What about *television*, *elephant* and *dinosaur*? What about those sentences your children write for themselves – they can extend to two pages if they include sufficient *and then's*! Incidentally, children appear to experience little difficulty with long sentences which are constructed from a series of co-ordinate clauses:

> She got up and had her breakfast and locked the door and went to school . . .

Short sentences like the following are obviously far more complex:

> The girl who had blonde hair got up.
>
> She had her breakfast after she had washed her hands.
>
> Before she had her breakfast, she washed her hands.

Although there will be a relationship between length of words/sentences and readability we need to know much more about the particular features of text which affect the reading fluency of primary age children.

Colin Harrison (1980) lists six broad headings:

- legibility of print
- illustration and colour
- vocabulary
- conceptual difficulty
- syntax
- organisation.

And Katherine Perera (1984) itemises five major causes of difficulty in text:

- physical – legibility etc.
- outside knowledge and experience
- unfamiliar vocabulary
- grammatical
- overall pattern of discourse organisation.

There is a marked similarity here and a conflation of Harrison's and Perera's headings will serve to structure further comment.

(1) *Physical*

This begins with the general attractiveness of the book, its cover and quality of illustration. Ensure that attractive books are displayed with their front covers visible whenever possible. Text and illustration should be complete on the page or facing pages. It has been found that where two or three lines of text are placed above an illustration with a large block of text below it, children often miss the shorter text. It is also helpful in the early stages if illustration then text appear in that order to encourage left-right, top-bottom orientation. Legibility seems an obvious variable but it includes factors like size and style of print, relationship between size of print and length of line and colour of print/colour of background. Some children's books have text over-printed onto the illustation and this often causes confusion if not complete word-blindness!

The point at which sentences (or words) are 'broken' when continuing onto the next line is often responsible for serious difficulty. Research (Raban, 1982) has now revealed that line-break (B) is less likely to disrupt fluency than line-break (A).

(A) She walked down the street
and went into a shop.

(B) She walked down the street and
went into a shop.

Trials with a large number of Year 6 Juniors revealed that words which are split at the end of a line, even at a syllable boundary, are likely to cause confusion, at least when reading aloud (Moon, 1979).

(2) *Previous experience*

Harrison (1980) illustrates this point by saying:

The phrase *a black hole in space* contains words which are in frequent use, and yet the concept to which it refers can only be fully understood by specialists in astro-physics. (p. 21)

Obviously readers can only comprehend what previous experience has prepared them for. They may be capable of decoding the words, or even reading the passage aloud but they can only be *reading* if they can match concepts to the language they see. Clearly this is another area which readability formulae could not begin to approach.

(3) *Vocabulary*

There have been various attempts to compile lists of words in common use – Dale's lists of 3000 and 769 words are examples. The formula procedure is then to count the number of unfamiliar words (words not in the lists) and compute a reading level (See Harrison, 1980, pp. 74–77 for details). Computer programs can take the strain nowadays but for most purposes teachers can assess familiarity of vocabulary by noting what their children are likely or unlikely to be able to read. Another time-saving device is to advise fluent readers how to carry out their own 'five-finger test'. This assumes approximately 100 words per page and requires the child to place a finger on each word she/he does not know ('unfamiliar vocabulary'). If children run out of fingers by the bottom of the page then the text is probably too hard for them. This derives from the 5 in 100 (or 5 per cent) accuracy ratio defined as the 'instructional level' of reading fluency.

(4) *Syntax*

This is probably the nearest we can get to the heart of readability but it is notoriously difficult to assess. The distinction between co-ordinate and subordinate sentence structures has already been made. Confusion in the early stages of learning to read has been noted with respect to pre-cued and post-cued speech:

Pre-cued: Joan said, 'I am going out.'
Post-cued: 'I am going out,' said Joan.

Reid (1970 explained that children get into difficulties with post-cued speech because it is almost entirely a feature of *written* language (of which they have limited experience) whereas pre-cued speech is almost always used in *oral* conversation. A further difficulty arises in dialogue if the post-cued speech becomes *Joan said*. Can you see why?

'I am going out,' Joan said,
'I will come with you,' said Sally.

Harrison (1980, p. 23) provides information about five types of difficulty related to syntax. For example he shows how active verbs are easier to read and recall than passive verbs:

The chairs were taken by the boys
is harder than
The boys took the chairs.

Katherine Perara claims that reading is likely to be harder when:

● the grammatical structure of a sentence is not easy to predict.
● a sentence does not divide readily into optimal segments for processing.
● a heavy burden is imposed on short-term memory.

See Perera (1984) pp. 280–317 for full details.

(5) *Organisation*

This is concerned with the way in which the whole text is written and presented. For example, Neate's (1988) 'structural guiders' are useful in non-fiction texts because they tell the reader what they can expect to find in the text. The use of bold or italicised type provides emphasis although it seems that young readers are more likely to emphasise what is printed in bold rather than in italics. Harrison again provides a detailed overview (pp. 25–28) and Perera (1984, pp. 317–325) discusses the advantages of stating the gist of a passage first and keeping to a strong sequential ordering of the material. She also asserts that the story frame is best, an echo of Barbara Hardy's 'narrative as a primary act of mind'. Certainly those

information books which are written in a narrative style (or 'story frame')
seem to be more accessible to novice readers presumably because that is the
style with which they are most familiar – in spoken *and* written language. At
first sight this appears to conflict with Bobbie Neate's assertion that 'a
straightfoward informational register is best'. In practice both positions are
tenable – it all depends on the child's previous experience and linguistic
development. Children with very little experience of information register
will find a narrative frame more accessible but as they are increasingly
exposed to information language (by hearing it read aloud) they will be able
to read it more confidently for themselves.

We recommend a useful summary of fifteen questions to ask of a text
provided by Beard (1990, p. 124) under five headings which correspond to
those presented above. They are phrased in such a way as to enable teachers
to use them as selection criteria without pre-supposing a great deal of
technical background knowledge.

Accessibility

Somewhat related to *organisation* is the ease with which a reader can 'get
into' a text and cope with its demands. It is akin to Neate's (1988) structural
guiders in information books but how are these paralleled in fiction books?
Warlow (1977) identified length of book and narrative structure as key
determinants of accessibility. Young children usually have a short
concentration span and, from a motivational point of view, it is desirable
that they should be able to complete a book in one sitting. Later they will be
able to leave off and pick up the story again but this will be easier to do if the
story is divided into manageable sections or short chapters. When they
become accomplished readers they will readily leave off reading several
times during the course of a long novel, their interest being sustained by the
intrinsic interest it has engendered. It is important to be aware of which
books are appropriate to different stages in the development of children's
reading stamina. This issue clearly relates to the way 'time for reading' is
organised within the classroom (See Chapter One) because classes or groups
cannot be expected to stop reading to order: saying 'Change over to your
next activity when you get to a good place to finish reading' *is better than
saying* 'Time to stop reading.'

Most picture books are designed to be read at a sitting but consider the
following sequence of fiction:

(1) *The Sniff Stories* (Whybrow, 1989. Ten separate stories about the same
      characters.

(2) *Under the Storyteller's Spell (Charles, 1989).* Eighteen separate stories
      by different authors.

(3)   *The Blood-and-Thunder Adventure on Hurricane Peak* (Mahy, 1989). Twenty-six short chapters, each developing an episode within a single novel.

Try developing this sequence, vertically *and* horizontally. Some novels make a dramatic impact on the first page, others do not get under way until chapter two or three. Some stories start at the end and flash back, after the second chapter. In *Mrs. Frisby and the Rats of NIMH* (O'Brien, 1972), for example, the beginning of the story (how the rats came to be as Mrs. Frisby found them) does not become apparent until Nicodemus starts to relate it to Mrs. Frisby almost half way through the book. Awareness of children's developing reading stamina and how this is affected by the different ways fictional books are structured deserves closer scrutiny especially by teachers of lower/middle juniors.

Summary

In this chapter we have attempted to demonstrate what the 'range of reading' strand in the National Curriculum might look like, so far as the provision of books is concerned, at Key Stages 1 and 2. We have related this emphasis to developments over the last twenty years and provided examples of the kinds of books which are necessary for implementation of the reading Attainment Target. We have also suggested some selection criteria for picture books, fiction, poetry, folk/fairy tales and non-fiction and finally outlined some of the major readability factors which apply to texts for primary-age children.

QUESTION

If you and your class were marooned on a desert island and allowed only twenty books, what would they be? Why?

CHAPTER 7

Where can I obtain further information about reading?

This closing chapter aims to outline *selected* sources of information about reading – information which will assist in the formulation, maintenance and future development of a school's reading policy. The information is grouped into eight main sections:

- Subscription journals and professional associations
- The Reading and Language Information Centre
- Packaged collections of children's books
- Radio and television broadcasts
- Computer software for developing reading
- Bookclubs
- Other useful information
- Books for teachers.

Finally we include a Reading Policy Checklist which has been designed to stimulate whole staff discussion about the issues raised in *A Question of Reading*.

Subscription journals and professional associations

Books for Keeps

Wealth of articles, author profiles and reviews. Published six times a year. Useful for Parents' Resource Area as well as teacher and child reference. Also published by Books for Keeps are two excellent Guides:

Poetry 0–16 edited by Morag Styles & Pat Triggs.
Green Guide to Children's Books edited by Richard Hill with introduction by Jonathon Porritt.

Details from: Books for Keeps, 6 Brightfield Road, Lee, London, SE12 8QF.

Children's Book Foundation

Operates a membership scheme which offers, for example:

- termly newsletters
- author profiles
- Author Bank Directory and Videos
- Book Week Handbook.

Details from: Children's Book Foundation, Book House, 45 East Hill, London, SW18 2QZ.

Language and Learning

Journal with excellent balance between theory and practice in attractive A4 format. Published three times a year (free to NATE members).

Details from: The Questions Publishing Company Ltd., 6/7 Hockley Hill, Hockley, Birmingham, B18 5AA.

National Association for the Teaching of English

Local branch meetings and annual national course/conference. Strong primary influence with good range of primary publications which are offered to members at reduced prices. Examples include:

> *Building a House of Fiction*
> *Children Reading to their Teachers*
> *Developing a Policy for Language*
> *Exploring Poetry 5-8*
> *Looking at Language in the Primary School*
> *Pictures on the Page.*

English in Education, the NATE journal, is published three times a year and is free to members (*Language and Learning* is also free to NATE primary members).

Details from: NATE Office, Birley High School, Fox Lane, Frecheville, Sheffield, S12 4WY.

School Library Association

Local branch meetings and bi-annual national conference. *The School Librarian* is the journal of the SLA and is published four times a year. It includes articles on librarianship and children's authors as well as a range of reviews under headings like:

Younger Readers
Seven to Eleven Fiction and Information Material
Five to Sixteen poetry and plays

The SLA has a good list of publications, available at reduced prices to members, a representative selection of which is listed below:

Barker, K. (1991) *Dick King-Smith*
Graham, J. & Plackett, E. (1987) *Developing Readers: Books to Encourage Children to Read*
Stephenson, C. (1990) *Feasts and Festivals*

Details from: The School Library Association, Liden Library, Barrington Close, Liden, Swindon SN3 6HF.

Signal

Journal, published three times a year by Thimble Press, for those with a serious interest in children's literature. Thimble Press also publishes inexpensive books about children's reading, a selection of which is listed below:

Bennett, J. (1991) *Learning to Read with Picture Books* (4th edition)
Chambers, A. (1991) *The Reading Environment*
Chambers, N. (1987) *Fiction 6-9*
Colwell, E. (1991) *Storytelling*
Meek, M. (1988) *How Texts Teach What Readers Learn*
Moss, E. (1988) *Picture Books for Young People 9-13*
Waterland, L. (1988) *Read With Me*

Details from: Thimble Press, Lockwood, Station Road, Woodchester, Stroud, Glos. GL5 5EQ.

United Kingdom Reading Association

Local branch meetings and an annual, national course/conference. The main journal is *Reading*, published three times a year in an illustrated A4 format and containing a wide range of articles by teachers, lecturers and researchers. For an additional subscription members can receive the UKRA's *Journal of Research in Reading*, a refereed journal published twice annually. UKRA also publishes a series of monographs:

Arnold, H. *Listening to Children Reading*
Beard, R. *Children's Writing in the Primary School*
Bloom, W. *Partnership with Parents*
Fisher, R. *Early Literacy and the Teacher*
Hall, N. *The Emergence of Literacy*
Mudd, N. *Let's Communicate*

Neate, B. *Finding Out about Finding Out*
Pumphrey, P. *Reading: Tests and Assessment Techniques*
Wray, D. *Teaching Information Skills through Project Work*

Details from: Administrative Secretary, UKRA, c/o Edge Hill College of Higher Education, St. Helen's Road, Ormskirk, Lancs.

Youth Libraries Group

Under the aegis of The Library Association, this organisation holds local meetings for librarians and teachers and publishes useful booklists and guides, a selection of which appears below:

Brown, R. & Willars, G. *Short Stories for Children*
Heaton, J. *Never Too Young*
Smythe, M. *Count Me In*
Video *Tell Me Another One*
Weir, L. *Telling the Tale*

Details from: Youth Libraries Group, Remploy, London Road, Newcastle under Lyme, Staffs. ST5 1RX.

The Reading and Language Information Centre

This used to be known as the Reading Centre and now occupies new premises at Bulmershe Court in Reading. Dr Viv Edwards was appointed Director in 1991 on the retirement of Betty Root who built up the Centre's reputation over many years. The Centre contains extensive collections and exhibitions of reading schemes, children's books and related resources, all attractively and spaciously displayed. Visitors are welcome throughout the year but they should telephone in advance of their visit. The Centre offers an extensive programme of whole-school in-service courses and conferences. It also operates a membership scheme which includes copies of current publications covering all aspects of the English/Language curriculum at Key Stages 1 & 2, a representative sample of which is listed below:

Assessing Reading at Key Stage 1 by Cliff Moon
Outlines facets of assessment required for Teacher Assessment and offers a simplified version of miscue analysis.

Creating a Handwriting Policy by Diana Bentley
Discusses issues to be covered when devising a handwriting policy.

Feelings by Cliff Moon
Annotated booklist of recently published paperback picture books and novels which explore children's emotions and relationships.

Group Reading in the Primary School by Diana Bentley and Anne Rowe
Looks at ways of including group reading in the curriculum.

Individualised Reading by Cliff Moon
Readability gradings of selected schemes, children's books, poetry, folk tales and non-fiction. Up-dated annually.

Learning to Read with Big Books by Pam Blewett
Rationale, organisation and use of big books in the classroom.

The Child, the Teacher and the National Curriculum
Four charts which provide practical help in delivery of National Curriculum 'English' at Key Stages 1 & 2.

Key Stage 1 Records, Key Stage 2 Records
Photocopiable record sheets for English: ATs 1-3. Pupil self-assessment profiles for each AT. These are closely related to The Child, the Teacher and the National Curriculum charts described above.

Stories for Time: Resourcing the History National Curriculum at Key Stage 1 by Chris Routh & Anne Rowe
Annotated book list.

Young Authors at Work by Viv Edwards and Angela Redfern
Describes the development of children's writing in the primary years and includes examples of practical activities.

VIDEO: Nobody Heard Me Read Today
Shows parents that 'reading aloud to teacher' is only *one* of the many ways reading is developed in school.

The Centre is also responsible for the AIMER (Access to Information on Multicultural Education Resources) data base. Lists of resources are available on a wide range of topics, from curriculum development to dual language books and from history to mathematics. An annual subscription entitles members to regular information updates.

Details from: Reading and Language Information Centre, University of Reading, Bulmershe Court, Earley, Reading, RG6 1HY. Tel: 0734 318820.

Packaged collections of children's books

A number of publishers and suppliers now market selections of boxed or film-wrapped children's books. Some, like *Picturemacs Packs* and *Puffin Library Bookshelves*, include paperbacks from a single publisher's list whereas *Badger Reading Boxes* and *Kaleidoscope* draw on titles from every children's book publisher. Others, like *Book Bus*, comprise books specifically commissioned by the publisher. A representative list of these packages appears below:

Badger Reading Boxes	Badger Books
Book Bus	Collins
Bookshelf	Harcourt Brace Jovanovich

Classroom Reading Packs	Corgi
Highgate	Harcourt Brace Jovanovich
Kaleidoscope	Books for Students
Picturemacs Packs	Macmillan
Puffin Library Bookshelves	Oliver & Boyd
Puffin Story Corner	Puffin
Read by Reading	Collins
Story Corner	Collins
Sunbeams Reading Packs	Heinemann
Viking Reading Boxes	Viking

The range of boxed collections produced by Books for Students deserves particular mention, partly because of their scope and partly because of the standard of their selection, presentation and teacher support material. They are a major supplier of books to schools, libraries and school bookshops and visitors are welcome to browse and order books at their purpose-built showroom in Warwick.

The Kaleidoscope range includes:

Kaleidoscope Reading Sets	Readability graded picture books and fiction compiled by Cliff Moon and directly related to *Individualised Reading* stages. 40 books per box.
Kaleidoscope Nursery/Reception Sets	Two boxes of 36 picture books compiled by Judith Elkin.
Kaleidoscope Picture Books 9–13	One box of 40 books compiled by Michael Jones.
Kaleidoscope Poetry Sets	One pack of 30 books at Key Stage 1, another at Key Stage 2 compiled by Michael Jones
Kaleidoscope Multicultural Sets	Mainly fiction which recognises a range of cultural/ethnic backgrounds. One set of 36 books at Key Stage 1, another at Key Stage 2, compiled by Judith Elkin.

Key Collections	Sets of up to 15 non-fiction titles to support National Curriculum themes:

KS1 Maths
     Science
     Environmental Education –
       Plants & Animals
     Geography

KS2 Science
     Environmental Education –
      About the Environment
     Environmental Education –
      Water
     Physical Geography
     History – Invaders & Settlers
     History – Tudors & Stuarts
     History – Exploration &
      Encounters

KS3 Geography

Details from: Books for Students, Bird Road, Heathcote, Warwick, CV34 6TB. Tel: 0926 314366.

Radio and television broadcasts

Radio

First Steps in Drama (7–9 years)
Uses drama to explore children's books.

Listening and Reading 1 & 2 (5–8 years); 3 (7–9 years)
Excellent selection of stories. Ideal for taping so that children can listen through headphones and follow the text simultaneously (pre-recorded cassettes and books are available through BBC/Longman).

Poetry Corner (5–7 years)
Miscellany of poems and rhymes, some set to music, with a weekly theme.

Wordplay (7–9 years)
Mixture of poems, rhymes and stories.

Verse Universe (9–12 years)
Miscellany of poems, quotations, tall tales, anecdotes, famous sayings and memorable speech.

148

BBC Television

English Express (9–11 years)
Explores writers and writing, starting with autobiography.

Look and Read (7–10 years)
Ten-part serialised story with accompanying children's booklets. Range of reading strategies, including phonics, in the centre 'teaching' slot.

Words and Pictures (5–7 years)
For children who have just started to read. Focal story presentation leads to initial letter phonics and prediction activities. Important to have the story books available for children to read after viewing.

You and Me Storytime (3–7 years)
Whole-curriculum series with an emphasis on stories.

ITV Television

Middle English (9–13 years)
Excellent series for upper juniors. Magazine format featuring authors, poets and serialisations of children's novels.

Picture Box (8–11)
Visual arts as well as stories of all kinds are featured. Good stimulus for creative work in the classroom.

Readabout (7–9 years)
Variety of presentations which introduce specific purposes for/modes of reading.

Storyworld (4–6 years)
A narrator creates two children in a fantasy world and then reviews his story's key words and phrases. Accompanying children's books of the stories.

Talk, Write and . . . Read (7–10 years)
Magazine format which features authors, poets and stories. A useful precursor to *Middle English*.

Computer software for developing reading

The programs which follow have been selected as good examples of a range of different computing approaches to reading development. They are meant to be indicative of the kind of software which primary teachers will find most useful.

Caption

(Micro Electronics Support Unit, Manchester Polytechnic, Hathersage Road, Manchester, M13 0AJ).

Provides opportunities for children who are less confident writers – contains a series of pictures and other graphic images with a space in each for children to enter short phrases or 'captions'. The printed pages can be very useful as reading material for children who are struggling with reading.

Developing Tray

(Capital Media, John Ruskin Street, London, SE5 0PQ).

A very flexible prediction activity which centres on deletions in text which can be generated by teacher or children. It is interactive and encourages syntactic awareness. There is also a simpler version called Infant Tray.

Dinosaur Discovery

(4Mation Educational Resources, Linden Lea, Rock Park, Barnstaple, Devon, EX32 9AQ).

An information-retrieval adventure game which involves children in reading a log in order to solve the problems which face them.

Fairy Tales

(Resource, Exeter Road, Off Coventry Grove, Doncaster, DN2 4PY).

Children are invited to build up their own fairy stories which are then published for other children to read. In effect this is an infant desk-top publishing package.

Front Page Extra

(Micros and Primary Education, Newman College Computer Centre, Bartley Green, Birmingham, B32 3NT).

Simple desk top publishing program which allows children to create news texts, with headings and sub-headings, in two or three columns. The published newspapers can then become useful resources for reading in the classroom.

150

News Bulletin

(Micros and Primary Education, Newman College Computer Centre, Bartley Green, Birmingham, B32 3NT).

Electronic bulletin board which introduces children to creating and reading teletext screens – provides opportunities for abbreviated styles of reporting *and* for readers to select further pages in order to retrieve information.

Police – Language in Evidence

(Cambridgeshire Software House, The Town Hall, St Ives, Huntingdon, Cambs).

A police station incident room simulation where precision is required in the use of language.

Touch Explorer Plus

(Micro Electronics Support Unit, Manchester Polytechnic, Hathersage Rd, Manchester, M13 8AJ).

Award-winning *concepts keyboard* based data handling package. Children can enter data at different levels of sophistication and readers can retrieve the material via the concept keyboard. It can also be used to explore narrative texts by using pictures to help sequence the story.

Wordplay

(BBC Publications, 35 Marylebone High Street, London, W1M 4AA).

Children enter nouns, verbs, adjectives etc and the program uses them to generate random phrases which can be used as starting points for descriptive prose or poetry as well as developing Knowledge about Language.

Bookclubs

Letterbox library

Suppliers of non-sexist and multicultural books for children. Book displays can be hired and a modest membership fee entitles schools to a newsletter and advice. The School Bookclub offers a selection of 20–30 books per term with a 10% discount on paperbacks.

Details from: Letterbox Library, FREEPOST 8 Bradbury Street, London N16 8BR.

Puffin Book Club

Six mailings a year of each of the *Post* (9-13 yrs), *Flight* (6-9 yrs) and *Fledgling* (0-6 yrs) lists. Children choose books they wish to buy – a card/stamp scheme is provided. Free copies of the Puffin Book Club magazines *Puffin Post* and *Puffin Flight* (normally 40p), as well as a one-hour audio tape are sent each term. Also provided are Teachers' Notes written by Jill Bennett, posters, free gifts etc. Every order entitles the school to 15 per cent of value in books and preview sets are offers at a 25 per cent discount. Book Weeks are also catered for and a free booklet *Classroom Activities for Bookweeks* is available.

Details from: Puffin Book Club, FREEPOST, 27 Wrights Lane, London, W8 5BR.

Red House Books

A children's/family book club – new lists are mailed every four weeks and only books which are ordered are sent to members. Lists contain hardbacks, paperback, audio and video cassettes at around 25 per cent discount. Recommended by the Pre-school Playgroups Association and well worth publicising in school.

Details from: The Red House, Witney, Oxon, OX8 5YF.

Scholastic Book Clubs

As well as *Criterion*, a book club for teachers and *Scene*, for secondary age children, there are three clubs for primary children:

See Saw	0-6 years
Lucky	7-9 years
Chip	9-12 years

At the beginning of each month in term time schools receive copies of the children's *Club News* which gives details of the books on offer. Requested books are then ordered and schools receive either free books or vouchers (one for every ten books ordered) *or* a 10 per cent cash discount. In addition Scholastic Book Fairs provide four selections of books in steel display cases:

Yellow Case	3-6 years
Green Case	6-9 years
Blue Case	9-12 years
Red Case	For advanced readers, parents & teachers

The school receives commission on Book Fair sales – either 50 per cent of takings in books, 25 per cent in cash *or* 25 per cent in books and 25 per cent in vouchers which can be redeemed against Scholastic Publications (e.g. Child/Junior Education, Bright Ideas series).

Details from: Scholastic Book Fairs, FREEPOST CV 1034, Westfield Road, Southam, Leamington Spa, Warks. CV33 0BR.

School Book Fairs Ltd

Over 300 books delivered to school for a one-week Fair. The school receives commission on sales – either 50 per cent of takings in books *or* 20 per cent in cash. Advance publicity provided and the collections of books are colour-coded as follows:

Yellow Selection	Picture and story books for beginner readers
Blue Selection	Story books for intermediate and good readers
Green Selection	Mainly non-fiction and activity books for all ages
Red Selection	Fiction and poetry for upper juniors

The company also runs a *Reading Awareness Scheme*.

Details from: School Book Fairs Ltd., FREEPOST, Priory Industrial Park, Christchurch, Dorset, BH23 4BR.

Other useful information

Big Books

The use of 'enlarged books' is recommended in the Programme of Study for Key Stage 1. They enable a group of children to see the text as it is read to them and the teacher can run a pointer along the print to *demonstrate* that it is the words, as well as the pictures, which convey the story. Several publishers now produce big books and the following are worth inspecting:

Book Bus Big Books	Collins
Bookshelf Big Books	Harcourt Brace Jovanovich
Giantsize Books	Kingscourt
Magic Beans Giant Books	Harcourt Brace Jovanovich
Oxford Reading Tree Big Books	O.U.P.
Readalong Rhythms Big Books	Mary Glasgow
Storychest Big Big Books	Nelson
Story Giants	Oliver & Boyd
Sunshine Big All Together Books	Heinemann

Note:

● A very useful guide to using Big Books in the classroom has been written by Pam Blewett (1991).

● Specially designed easel type stands for holding Big Books are available from: Kilokrafts, Unit 5, Tollgate Estate, Stanbridge Earls, Nr. Romsey, Hants.

Professional Storytellers

Visiting storytellers often provide a stimulus for reading traditional stories as well as introducing children to a variety of narrative forms. The following selection illustrates the range of available agencies:

Common Lore Storytelling Company Ltd.
In addition to providing storytellers this group also produces a resource pack of audio tape and booklet on classroom activities.

Details from: Brixton Enterprise Centre (Unit 132), Bonmarche Building, 444 Brixton Road, London, SW9 8EJ.

Company of Storytellers
This group includes Pomme Clayton, Godfrey Duncan-Tuup, Ben Haggarty, Daisy Keable and High Lupton.

Details from: Hugh Lupton, 8 Church Terrace, Aylsham, Norfolk, NR11 6EU.

Flora and Tuup
Godfrey Duncan-Tuup tells Afro-Carribean, Middle Eastern and Asian stories alongside Flora Gatha, a classical Indian dancer.

Details from: Flat 70, Charles Hawking House, Bollo Bridge Road, Acton, London W3.

Kabutar Shadow Puppet Company
Presents stories and puppets as well as running workshops for children and teachers. Tales from Jatakas, the stories of the rebirths of Lord Buddha, are often performed as are songs in both Hindi and English.

Details from: 137a Kensington High Street, London, W8 6SU.

Tamba Roy
Presents Jamaican heritage.

Details from: 51 Salford Road, Streatham Hill, London, SW2 4BL.

Readathon

A national sponsored reading event in aid of the Malcolm Sargent Cancer Fund for Children and which, since its foundation in 1987, has raised over

£3 million and helped over 15,000 children. The Princess of Wales is Patron and many prominent children's authors pledge support each year. It is organised by Books for Students and held in schools and public libraries as part of Children's Book Week. Children undertake to read a certain number of books during a specified period – usually a week or fortnight encompassing Book Week or at any time during the Autumn Term.

Details from: Readathon Office, Books for Students Ltd., Bird Road, Heathcote, Warwick. CV34 6TB.

Tapes and Videos

There are a number of excellent audio and video tapes available which feature children's books or authors. The following are notable for their presentation quality:

Authorbank Videos,	Children' Book Foundation
Cover to Cover (audio tapes),	Puffin
Favourite Stories from Words and Pictures (video tapes),	BBC Enterprises
Higgledy Humbug and Popcorn Pie (audio tapes),	Mary Glasgow
Listening and Reading 1–3 (audio tapes),	BBC/Longman
Tapeworm Children's Cassettes,	Tapeworm Cassettes Ltd, Apsley House, Apsley Road, New Malden, Surrey, KT3 3NJ.
Weston Woods (audio & video),	Weston Woods, 14 Friday Street, Henley-on-Thames, Oxon.

Books for Teachers

(a) *Pre-National Curriculum Books*

Arnold, H. (1982), *Listening to Children Reading*, London: Hodder & Stoughton.
Ashworth, E. (1988) *Language Policy in the Primary School*, London: Croom Helm.
Benton, M. & Fox, G. (1985) *Teaching Literature Nine-Fourteen*, Oxford: Oxford University Press.
Bloom, W. (1988) *Managing to Read: A Whole School Approach to Reading*, London: Mary Glasgow.
Clark, M. M. ed., (1985) *New Directions in the Study of Reading*, London: Falmer Press.
C.L.P.E. (1988) *The Primary Language Record*, London: Centre for Language in Primary Education.

Hall, N. (1987) *The Emergence of Literacy*, London: Hodder & Stoughton.

Martin, T. (1989) *The Strugglers*, Milton Keynes: Open University Press.

Meek, M. (1982) *Learning to Read*, London: The Bodley Head.

Meek, M. & Mills, C. (1988) *Language and Literacy in the Primary School*, London: Falmer Press.

Pearson, H. (1987) *Children Becoming Readers*, Basingstoke: Macmillan.

Southgate, V. *et al*. (1981) *Extending Beginning Reading*, London: Heinemann for Schools Council.

Tavener, D. (1980) *Developing a Reading Programme*, London: Ward Lock Educational.

(b) *Post-National Curriculum Books*

Beard, R. (1990) *Developing Reading 3–13 (2nd edition)*, London: Hodder & Stoughton.

Cairney, T. H. (1990) *Teaching Reading Comprehension: Meaning Makers at Work*, Milton Keynes: Open University Press.

Carter, R. ed. (1990) *Knowledge About Language*, London: Hodder & Stoughton.

C.L.P.E. (1990) *Patterns of Learning*, London: Centre for Language in Primary Education.

D.E.S. (1990) *The Teaching and Learning of Language and Literacy*, London: HMSO.

Hutchinson, D. & Pigeon, S. (1991) *Teaching English in the Primary Curriculum*, Oxford: Blackwell.

Pumphrey, P. (1991) *Improving Children's Reading in the Junior School*, London: Cassell.

Tann, S. (1991) *Developing Language in the Primary Classroom*, London: Cassell.

Tavener, D. (1990) *Reading Within and Beyond the Classroom*, Milton Keynes: Open University Press.

Wray, D. & Medwell, J. (1991) *Literacy and Language in the Primary Years*, London: Routledge.

Reading policy checklist

The following checklist serves two purposes:

- Summary of issues raised in *A Question of Reading*
- Suggested basis of a primary school's reading policy

Class organisation/management   *Chapter 1*

- classroom arrangement
- curriculum management
- resource management
- people management
- space management

156

- radio and TV broadcasts
- computer software
- book clubs
- big books
- other means of support

References to Children's Books

Ahlberg, J. & Ahlberg. A. (1977) *Jeremiah in the Dark Woods*, London: Kestrel.
Ahlberg, J. & Ahlberg, A. (1978) *Each Peach Pear Plum*, London: Kestrel.
Armitage, R. & D. (1977) *The Lighthouse Keeper's Lunch*, London, Deutsch.
Bradman, T. & Dupasquier, P. (1989) *The Sandal*, London: Andersen Press.
Bucknall, C. (1987) *One Bear in the Picture*, London: Macmillan.
Burningham, J. (1970) *Mr Gumpy's Outing*, London: Jonathon Cape.
Butterworth, N. & Inkpen, M. (1990) *The School Trip*, London: Hodder & Stoughton.
Charles, F. Ed., (1989) *Under the Storyteller's Spell: Folk-tales from the Caribbean*, London: Viking Kestrel.
Ehrlich, A. (1986) *The Walker Book of Fairy Tales*, London: Walker Books.
Fine, A. (1989) *Goggle-Eyes*, London: Hamish Hamilton.
Garner, A. (1984) *Book of British Fairy Tales*, London: Collins.
Guenier, E. (1991) *Can You Keep a Secret?* London: Harper Collins.
Hill, E. (1980) *Where's Spot?* London: Heinemann.
Hutchins, P. (1970a) *The Surprise Party*, London: The Bodley Head.
Hutchins, P. (1970b) *Rosie's Walk*, London: The Bodley Head.
Hutchins, P. (1976) *Don't Forget the Bacon*, London: The Bodley Head.
Hutchins, P. (1990) *Which Witch is Which?* London: Julia MacRae.
King-Smith, D. (1985) *Saddlebottom*, London: Victor Gollancz.
Lively, P. (1976) *A Stitch in Time*, London: Heinemann.
MacKay, D., Thompson, B. & Schaub, P. (1970) *Breakthrough to Literacy*, Harlow: Longman.
Mahy, M. (1989) *The Blood-and-Thunder Adventure on Hurricane Peak*, London: Dent.
Mayhew, J. (1991) *Katie and the Dinosaurs*, London: Orchard Books.
Moon, C. (1988) *The Twelve Dancing Princesses* (*Once upon a Time series*), Aylesbury: Ginn.
Nicoll, H. & Pienkowski, J. (1973) *Meg and Mog*, London: Heinemann.
O'Brien, E. (1988) *Tales for the Telling: Irish Folk and Fairy Stories*, Harmondsworth: Puffin.
O'Brien, R. (1972) *Mrs Frisby and the Rats of NIMH*, (sometimes re-titled *The Secret of NIMH*) London: Victor Gollancz.
Riordan, J. (1983) *Tales from the Arabian Nights*, London: Hamlyn.
Whybrow, I. (1989) *The Sniff Stories*, London: The Bodley Head.

158

References

Adams, M. J. (1991) *Beginning to Read: Thinking and learning about print*, Cambridge Mass.: MIT Press.

Arnold, H. (1982) *Listening to Children Reading*, London: Hodder & Stoughton.

ASE (1989) *The National Curriculum - making it work for the primary school*. Hatfield: ASE/ATM/MA/NATE.

Baker, A. (1984) 'Dawn Reads to her Teacher' in NATE Primary Committee, *Children Reading to their Teachers*, Sheffield: NATE, pp. 7-15.

Baker, A. (1985) 'Developing Reading with Juniors' in Moon, C. (ed.) *Practical Ways to Teach Reading*, London: Ward Lock Educational, pp. 16-26.

Bamberger, R. (1976) 'Literature and Development of Reading' in Merritt, J. E. (ed.) *New Horizons in Reading*, Newark, Delaware: International Reading Association.

Beard, R. (1990) *Developing Reading 3-13*, 2nd edition, London: Hodder & Stoughton.

Bennett, J. (1979) *Learning to Read with Picture Books*, 1st edition, Stroud: The Thimble Press.

Bentley, D. & Rowe, A. (1991) *Group Reading in the Primary Classroom*, University of Reading: Reading and Language Information Centre.

Benton, M. & Fox, G. (1985) *Teaching Literature Nine to Fourteen*, Oxford: Oxford University Press.

Bishop, D. & Adams, C. (1990) 'A prospective study of the relationship between specific language impairment, phonological disorders and reading retardation' in *Journal of Child Psychology and Psychiatry* 31.7, pp. 1027-1050.

Blewett, P. (1991) *Learning to Read with Big Books*, Reading: Reading and Language Information Centre, Reading University.

Bruner, J. S. (1957) 'On perceptual readiness' in *Psychological Review*, **64**, pp. 123-152.

Bruner, J. S. (1984) 'Language, Mind and Reading' in Goelman, H., and Oberg, A. & Smith, F. (eds) *Awakening to Literacy*, London, Heinemann.

Bryant, P. & Bradley, L. (1985) *Children's Reading Problems*, Oxford: Basil Blackwell.

Cairney, T. H. (1990) *Teaching Reading Comprehension: Meaning Makers at Work*. Milton Keynes: Open University Press.

Cane, B. & Smithers, J. (1971) *The Roots of Reading*, Slough: NFER.

Campbell, R. (1988) *Hearing Children Read*, London: Routledge.

Chall, J. S., Jacobs, V. A. & Baldwin, L. E. (1990) *The Reading Crisis: why poor children fail*, Cambridge Mass.: Harvard University Press.

Chaney, C. (1989) 'I pledge a legiance to the flag: three studies of word segmentation' in *Applied Psycholinguistics* **10**, pp. 261-281.

Chomsky, N. (1957) *Aspects of a Theory of Syntax*, Cambridge Mass.: MIT Press.
C.L.P.E. (1988) *The Primary Language Record*, London: Centre for Language in Primary Education.
Clarke, M. (1976) *Young Fluent Readers*, London: Heinemann.
Clay, M. M. (1975) *What Did I Write?* London: Heinemann.
Clay, M. M. (1979a) *Reading: the patterning of complex behaviour* (2nd ed.) London: Heinemann.
Clay, M. M. (1979b) *The Early Detection of Reading Difficulties: a diagnostic survey with recovery procedures* (revised ed.) London: Heinemann.
Clay, M. M. (1985) *The Early Detection of Reading Difficulties*, 3rd edition, London: Heinemann.
Clay, M. M. (1987) 'Implementing reading recovery: systematic adaptations to an educational innovation' in *New Zealand Journal of Educational Studies* 22.1 pp. 35–58.
Clay, M. M. (1991) *Becoming Literate: the construction of inner control*, Auckland NZ: Heinemann.
Cronbach, J. J. (1977) *Educational Psychology* (3rd ed.) New York: Harcourt Brace.
DES (1965) *Children and their Primary Schools*, London, HMSO.
DES (1975) *A Language for Life*, London: HMSO.
DES (1988) *Report of the Committee of Enquiry into Teaching of the English Language: The Kingman Report*, London: HMSO.
DES/WO (1988a) *National Curriculum: Task Group on Assessment and Testing: A Report* London: HMSO.
DES/WO (1988b) *English for Ages 5 to 11*, London: HMSO.
DES/WO (1989a) *English for Ages 5 to 16*, London: HMSO.
DES/WO (1989b) *English in the National Curriculum* (*No. 1*) London: HMSO.
DES/WO (1990) *English in the National Curriculum* (*No. 2*) London: HMSO.
Donaldson, M. (1989) *Sense and Sensibility: some thoughts on the teaching of literacy*, Occasional Paper No. 3 Reading: Reading and Language Information Centre, University of Reading.
Donaldson, M. & Reid, J. (1987) 'Language Skills in Reading' in Hendry, A. (ed.) *Teaching Reading: The Key Issues*, London: Heinemann.
Downing, J. (1973) *Comparative Reading*, New York: Macmillan.
Dougill, P. & Knott, R. (1988) *The Primary Language Book*, Milton Keynes: Open University Press.
Education, Science and Arts Committee (1991) *Standards of Reading in Primary Schools*, London: HMSO.
EHRI, L. (1979) 'Linguistic Insight: threshold of reading acquisition' in Waller, T. G. & MacKinnon, G. E. (ed.) *Reading Research: Advances in Theory and Practice*, New York: Academic Press.
Ferreiro, E. & Teberosky, A. (1983) *Literacy Before Schooling*, London: Heinemann.
Francis, H. (1982) *Learning to Read: literate behaviour and orthographic knowledge*, London: George Allen & Unwin.
Gawith, G. (1987) *Library Alive!* London: A & C. Black.
Gawith, G. (1990) *Reading Alive!* London: A & C. Black.
Great Britain (1988) *The Education Reform Act*.
Gray, J. (1979) 'Reading progress in English infant schools: some problems emerging from a study of teacher effectiveness' in *British Educational Research Journal* 5.2, pp. 141–157.

Gray, J. (1981) 'School effectiveness research: key issues' in *Educational Research* 24.1, pp. 49–54.

Goodacre, E. (1976) 'Miscue Analysis' in Longley, C. (ed.) *Teaching Young Readers*, London: BBC Publications.

Goodman, K. S. (1973) 'Miscues: Windows on the Reading Process' in Goodman, K. S. (ed.) *Miscue Analysis, Applications to Reading Instruction*, ERIC, Urbana Ill., pp. 3–14.

Goodman, Y. & Burke, C. (1972) *Reading Miscue Inventory*, London: Collier Macmillan.

Hannon, P. & James, S. (1990) 'Parents' and teachers' perspectives on pre-school literacy development' in *British Educational Research Journal* 16.3, pp. 259–272.

Harrison, C. (1980) *Readability in the Classroom*, Cambridge: Cambridge University Press.

Heath, S. B. (1983) *Ways with Words*, Cambridge: CUP.

HMI (1989) *Reading Policy and Practice at Ages 5–14*. London: DES.

HMI (1990) *The Teaching and Learning of Reading in Primary Schools*, London: DES.

Hill, L. E. (1978) 'A readability study of school library provision related to children's interests and reading abilities' Unpublished dissertation, University of London Institute of Education.

Holdaway, D. (1979) *The Foundations of Literacy*, Sydney: Aston Scholastic.

Hodgson, J. & Pryke, D. (1983) Reading Competence at 6 and 10: *A survey of styles of teaching reading in twenty Shropshire primary schools*, Shrewsbury: Shropshire County Council.

Hynds, J. (1988) 'The Great Debate about Reading – in pursuit of a little understanding' in *Books for Keeps*, No. 52, pp. 4–5.

Johnson, P. (1990) *A Book of One's Own*, London: Hodder & Stoughton.

Lake, M. (1991) 'Surveying all the factors: reading research' in *Language and Learning* 6, pp. 8–13.

Lundberg, I., Frost, J. & Peterson, O.P. (1988) 'Effects of an extensive programme for stimulating phonological awareness in pre-school children' in *Reading Research Quarterly* 23.3 pp. 264–284.

Luke, A. (1988) *Literacy, Textbooks and Ideology*, London: Falmer Press.

Lunzer, E. & Gardner, K. (1979) *The Effective Use of Reading*, London: Heinemann for Schools Council.

Lunzer, E. & Gardner, K. (1984) *Learning from the Written Word*, Edinburgh: Oliver & Boyd for Schools Council.

Mason, J. M. (1980) 'When do children begin to read?: an exploration of four-year-old children's letter and word competences' in *Reading Research Quarterly* 15.2, pp. 203–227.

Mason, J. (1990) 'The development of concepts about written language in the first three years of schooling' in *British Journal of Educational Psychology* 60, pp. 266–283.

Meek, M., Warlow, A. & Barton, G. (1977) *The Cool Web*, London: The Bodley Head.

Meek, M. (1982) *Learning to Read*, London: The Bodley Head.

Meek, M. (1988) *How Texts Teach What Readers Learn*, Stroud: The Thimble Press.

Meyer, L. A. (1983) 'Increased student achievement in reading: one district's strategies' in *Research in Rural Education* 45.3, pp. 28–31.

Michaels, W. & Walsh, M. (1990) *Up and Away: Using Picture Books*, Oxford: Oxford University Press.

Moon, C. (1979) 'Categorisation of miscues arising from textual weakness' in Thackray, D. (ed.) *Growth in Reading*, London, Ward Lock Educational, pp. 135–146.

Moon, C. (1984) 'Making use of miscues when children read aloud' in NATE Primary Committee, *Children Reading to their Teachers*, Sheffield: NATE, pp. 19–21.

Moon, C. (1986) 'Spot and Pat: Living in the best company when you read' in Root, B. (ed.) *Resources for Reading – Does Quality Count?* Basingstoke: Macmillan pp. 34–46; Reprinted in *Gnosis 13*, 1988.

Moon, C. (1992) *Individualised Reading* (23rd edition), University of Reading: Reading and Language Information Centre.

Moon, C. & Wells, G. (1979) 'Influence of the home on learning to read' in *Journal of Research in Reading* 2.1, pp. 53–62.

Morris, J. M. (1966) *Standards and Progress in Reading*, Slough: NFER.

NCC (1989) *English Non-Statutory Guidance No. 1*, York: NCC.

NCC (1990) *English Non-Statutory Guidance No. 2*. York: NCC.

Nash, I. (1989) 'Unlikely to accept coming second in endurance test' in *Times Educational Supplement* 4 Aug., p. 8.

Neate, B. (1988) 'Children's Information Books' in *Gnosis 13*, pp. 42–46.

Paice, S. (1985) 'Reading and Learning' in Moon, C. (ed.) *Practical Ways to Teach Reading*, London: Ward Lock Educational.

Perera, K. (1984) *Children's Writing and Reading*, Oxford: Blackwell.

Piaget, J. (1955) *The Child's Construction of Reality*, London: Routledge & Kegan Paul.

Pryke, D. (1991) *Primary School Study Reading*, Shropshire: Language Centre, Shrewsbury.

Raban, B. (1979) 'Do teachers make a difference?' in Thackray, D. (ed.) *Growth in Reading* London: Ward Lock.

Raban, B. (1982) 'Text display effects on the fluency of young readers' in *Journal of Research in Reading*, Vol. 5, No. 1, pp. 7–27.

Raban, B. (1984) *Observing Children Learning to Read and Write*, Unpublished Ph.D. thesis, University of Reading.

Reed, B. D. (1990) 'Reading: "high status" rhetoric and "low status" reality' in *Reading* 24:1, pp. 15–20.

Reid, J. (1970) 'Sentence structure in reading primers' in *Research in Education*, Vol. 3, pp. 23–37.

SEAC (1991) *Handbook of Guidance for the SAT, Teachers' Book and Assessment Record Booklet*, all at Key Stage 1, London: HMSO.

Short, H. (1989) *Bright Ideas: Using Books in the Classroom*, Leamington Spa: Scholastic.

Somerfield, M., Torbe, M., & Ward, C. (1983) *A Framework for Reading: Creating a Policy in the Primary School*, London: Heinemann for Coventry LEA.

Southgate, V. (1970) 'The importance of structure in beginning reading' in Gardner, K. (ed.) *Reading Skills: Theory and Practice*, London: Ward Lock.

Southgate, V., Arnold, H., & Johnson, S. (1981) *Extending Beginning Reading*, London: Heinemann for Schools Council.

Snow, C. E., Barnes W. S., Chandler, J., Goodman, I. F. & Hemphill, L. (1991) *Unfulfilled Expectations: Home and school influences on literacy*, Cambridge Mass.: Harvard University Press.

Spencer, M. (1976) 'Stories are for telling' in *English in Education*, Vol. 10, No. 1, pp. 16–23.

162

Stallings, J. A. (1976) 'How instructional processes relate to child outcomes in a national study of "Follow Through" ' in *Journal of Teacher Education* 27.1, pp. 43–47.

Stanovich, K. (1986) 'Matthew effects in reading: some consequencies of individual differences in the acquisition of literacy' in *Reading Research Quarterly* 21.4, pp. 360–406.

Sykes, J. B. ed. (1976) *The Concise Oxford Dictionary of Current English* (6th edition) Oxford: OUP.

Tann, S. (Ed.) (1988) *Developing Topic Work in the Primary School*, London: Falmer Press.

Thompson, B. (1970) *Learning to Read*, London: Sidgwick & Jackson.

Tunmer, W. & Nesdale, A. R. (1985) 'Phonemic segmentation skill and beginning reading' in *Journal of Educational Psychology* 77, pp. 417–427.

Vernon, M. D. (1971) *Reading and its Difficulties*, Cambridge: CUP.

Wade, B. (Ed.) (1990) *Reading for Real*, Milton Keynes: Open University Press.

Warlow, A. (1977) 'Reading and Readability' in *Language Matters* Vol. 2, No. 3, London: Centre for Language in Primary Education.

Waterland, L. (1985) *Read with Me* (1st edition), Stroud: The Thimble Press.

Waterland, L. (1988) *Read with Me* (2nd edition), Stroud: The Thimble Press.

Wells, G., Barnes, S. & Wells, J. (1984) *Linguistic Influences on Educational Attainment*, Final Report to DES Home and School Influences on Educational Attainment Project, University of Bristol.

Winkworth, E. (1977) *User Education in Schools: A survey of the literature on education for library and information use in schools*, London: British Library Research & Development Department.

Wiseman, S. (1968) 'Educational deprivation and disadvantage' in Butcher, H. J. (ed.) *Educational Research in Britain Vol 1* London: London University Press.

Wray, D. (1985) *Teaching Information Skills Through Project Work*, London: Hodder & Stoughton.

Wray, D. (1988) *Project Teaching* (Bright Ideas Management Books) Leamington Spa: Scholastic.

Index